Photo: Jamie Dunbar

ALANA VALENTINE's writing has been awarded the 2003 NSW Writer's Fellowship, the 2002 Rodney Seaborn Playwrights' Award and an International Writing Fellowship at Shakespeare's Globe Theatre in London. She also received a 2001 commendation for the Louis Esson Prize, a 1999 AWGIE Award, a residency at the Banff Playwrights' Conference in Canada, the ANPC/New Dramatists Award in New York City, a Churchill Fellowship for England and Ireland and a NSW Premier's Award.

Her stage plays include *Swimming the Globe* (1996), *The Conjurers* (1997), *Ozone* and *Spool Time* (1998), *Row of Tents* and *The Prospectors* (2001), *The Story of Anger Lee Bredenza* and *The Mapmaker's Brother* (2002), *Radio Silence, Savage Grace* and *Titania's Boy* (2003) and *Run Rabbit Run* (2004).

From left: Josef Ber (partly obscured) as Mark Courtney, Eliza Logan as Nolene Piggins, Wayne Blair (foreground) as Nicholas Pappas and Julie Hamilton as Barbara Selby in the 2004 Company B production in Sydney. (Photo:Heidrun Löhr)

RUN RABBIT RUN
Alana Valentine

Currency Press, Sydney

CURRENCY PLAYS

Run Rabbit Run first published in 2004
by Currency Press Pty Ltd,
PO Box 2287, Strawberry Hills, NSW, 2012, Australia
enquiries@currency.com.au
www.currency.com.au

All quotes from News Limited publications and the News Corporation Annual Report are gratefully used with News Limited's permission.

In accordance with the requirement of the Australian Media, Entertainment & Arts Alliance, Currency Press has made every effort to identify, and gain permission of, the artists who appear in the photographs which illustrate these plays.

NATIONAL LIBRARY OF AUSTRALIA CIP DATA
    Valentine, Alana, 1961–.
       Run rabbit run.
       ISBN 0 86819 747 5.
       1. South Sydney Rugby League Football Club – Drama. 2. Rugby football teams – Drama. I. Title. (Series: Currency plays).
    A822.3

Publication of this title was assisted by the Commonwealth Government through the Australia Council, its arts funding and advisory body.

Set by Dean Nottle
Printed by Hyde Park Press, Richmond, SA
Cover design by Kate Florance
Front cover photo shows Julie Hamilton as Barbara Selby and Josef Ber as Mark Courtney in the 2004 Company B production in Sydney. (Photo: Heidrun Löhr)

FOREWORD

To find myself writing this foreword to the published edition of Alana Valentine's compelling script for *Run Rabbit Run* is curious indeed.

I was just another fan when South Sydney was so unceremoniously dumped from the competition on 15 October 1999. Five days later, through a combination of luck and perseverance, I was given the task of leading the legal challenge aimed at securing the Club's reinstatement. And now, almost five years later, with Souths' place in the competition again secure, I look back upon those times and wonder just what could have happened had not a community risen, almost as one, to stop a great wrong.

I think now of the sacrifices George Piggins and others around him made while the legal battle dragged on. I think of those thousands of faceless fans who gave from their pockets and from their hearts to see preserved something that they rightly felt should not be taken away. And I think of those many more people beyond the world of Rugby League who were moved by a story that symbolised in eloquent terms the struggle of community against big business.

The South Sydney story, its many twists and turns, is beautifully evoked in Alana's skilful interweaving of the contemporary dialogue of the various participants. Upon first viewing, I was struck just how 'close to the bone' the drama became, as Alana deftly moved her spotlight from character to character. From the impassioned pleas of contrasting celebrities Andrew Denton and Alan Jones, to the defiant expressions of outrage from feisty Norm Lipson and Jimmy Lahood, the events of those manic days come to life.

And connecting it all are the wonderful words of the common fan—people like Mark Courtney, Phillip Pike, Greg Wilkinson, Eileen McLaughlin, Barbara Selby and her daughter Marcia. It is they, along with many others, who were the lifeblood of the fightback, and they constitute the cement that binds together this engaging playscript.

There are many lessons to be learned from this story—one only hopes that those who need to learn most are reading on…

Nicholas Pappas
Chairman, South Sydney Rabbitohs

for my grandmother, Joyce Wainwright,
who took me to my first football match

Contents

A BRIDGE FROM SPORT TO ART

In January 2004, when you walked into the Upstairs theatre at Belvoir Street, in Sydney's Surry Hills, things suddenly became very busy. Sure, in the foyer and on your way up the stairs you were surrounded by 350-odd people keen to find their seats and settle in for a night at the theatre. It was an urge swiftly tempered on entering the theatre space, however, by the walls. People's attention was drawn away from the bench seating, the ushers, the stage covered in live turf, even the occasional celebrity friend of the Rabbitohs, by a profusion of images. Almost every inch of the walls, on-stage and beyond, all the way around the auditorium in fact, was covered in photographs, cartoons and portraits of the South Sydney Rugby League Football Club. Where to look? What to do? Sit or browse?

For some of the audience these pictures were simply nameless faces with funny hair cuts on yellowing paper, beefy blokes tossing balls around—but for many others they were heroes, legends, rolemodels, idols, gods. Brian Thomson, the designer, and the Company B production team, had asked the community to dig deep for old photos or memorabilia, and they had offered Company B the most extraordinary collection, now literally spilling from the stage to engulf the entire wall space. As the house lights faded Mark Howett's lighting design caught these faces and moments in sharp specials of light whizzing around the Belvoir cauldron, ushering the actors on stage.

It was a terrific moment, not simply because it was unexpected (and introduced us to some Souths personalities), but because it suggested that there was more to this tale than just footy. It hinted at a complex world of generosity and pride, heavy with the past, pageantry, portents, crunch moments and bodies straining to be the best. Did it also suggest an evening of hagiography, partisanship and blind acceptance of simplistic iconographies and antagonisms? The joy of good theatre is that such an approach would have been against the very nature of the theatrical event. Theatre thrives on conflict and cries out for diverging points of view and personalities, both misty-eyed and on the warpath. And this story, unsurprisingly, had them all in spades.

Of course, the production went on to give the profusion of Souths images a visceral topography, historical context and a muscular, prolix and occasionally inarticulate embodiment. It did this entirely with the actual voices of many of those who played in the saga itself. As a result, here is plain-talking, fury, pride, hypocrisy, pathos, bathos and gallows humour as the last of the Sydney community footy teams stood up for itself and, David-like, defeated Goliath. Here is corporeal, manual history. A play about a community's voice, spoken by those very voices, with gall and audacity.

Run Rabbit Run is not just a play about an underdog footy team, or about enfranchising forgotten or repressed voices (although this story generated reams of commentary, some of which made it into the play). It is about making history, not its dramatisation or lateral fictionalisation, but an authentic chunk of the coalface: the words, deeds and confessions of people who sought to make a difference. From the grass roots to the corporate and celebrity high-fliers, from the driven fans to the actual power-brokers, from old players and coaches to the mother and daughter team cutting up faulty stickers, here was a story beyond football, a quest, perhaps futile, for autonomy, self-respect and fair play. Or, as Alana was wont to say, a play about moral courage.

Here are real characters, both Davids and Goliaths, some with dignity, others wearing their venality on their sleeve, some with stinging observations on Australian society, and yet more with heartbreaking tales of loss and self-sacrifice. What would people forfeit to stand up for what they believed was right? How much would people stake on seeing justice done? And anyway, what is justice in the murky worlds of corporate law and trade practices? This play slices to the very heart of inner urban Australia, its duelling concerns of entertainment and business, Mammon and local integrity, perceptions of old Australia and something altogether new. This play attempts to document the spirit of the Rabbitohs, something News Limited, among others, dismissed as essentially meaningless as they sought to change the face of Rugby League in Australia. If it can't be quantified, bought and traded, can it really be said to exist?

Chances are that anyone who lived in Sydney during the late 1990s knew something of the story of the Rabbitohs. When Rugby League was created, and the competition launched, Souths were a foundation club. Drawn from a densely populated series of working-class suburbs just south of the city of Sydney, it was a club with a proud tradition, dominating the game, most particularly in the late 1960s and early 1970s. Yet they had fallen from grace. In recent years they floundered close to the bottom of the table. As commercial imperatives dictated the future of the game, under-performing clubs faced the axe. Some clubs merged, but Souths tried to go it alone and ended being excluded from the first grade competition. Unwilling to lie down and die, the club and its supporters fought back and became a cause célèbre, drawing many in their wake as they took on a multinational company and the game's administrators in the name of their community, the underdog Aussie Battler and the Red and the Green. In the end, of course, they won, but not before much hyperbole and some of the biggest sporting rallies in history, plus the support of some heavyweights of Australian society and culture.

Theatrically this project had much to offer. Of course there were the human stories of heroism and pig-headedness, sadness and hilarity. A play of this nature also seemed to say something about the importance of sport in our culture, and the value and self-respect of a certain community within the wider Australian cultural landscape. Beyond this it offered a powerful theatrical trope, keying in to some fundamental cultural archetypes: clutching life from death; global capital versus community; a normally disparate community coming together through action; and the effective power of many voices.

Both Alana and I also had more personal connections to the story. Declaring our interest upfront, we well knew, at close quarters, both the team's tradition and the lie of the land. I had worked in a pub in Sydney's Waterloo for many years in my early twenties, serving schooner after schooner (usually Reschs, the beer we drink round here) to ex-players and garbos, hearing stories of the glory days, of mad exploits on and off the field. For Alana, though, Souths was a family team. She grew up in Sydney's south (really Dragons territory), but her grandparents were Souths fans (her grandfather played with Souths Juniors) so Souths was always her team.

After discussing the idea at the Australian National Playwrights' Conference in 2002 when we worked together on another of her plays, Alana later, more formally, pitched the Rabbitohs play to me at a café on the border of Surry Hills and Redfern. Concerned that no theatre would pick up a play about footy, she spoke passionately. Not only was this a story of a bunch of sports fans winning against the odds, but it could also be a piece of theatre about the determination and fearlessness, courage and love, and misplaced allegiances and hopes of real people, trying to understand and re-fashion their community. At a programming meeting for Company B Neil Armfield raised his eyebrows at the prospect of the play and Alana was commissioned to give us a taste of the voices out there.

The project fitted snugly with Company B's longer-term artistic strategy to engage more fully with the community at its doorstep. Belvoir Street Theatre is located opposite a massive housing commission tower block and is less than three kilometres from the newish home of the Rabbitohs in Redfern (not far, indeed from the home of Currency Press!). It is in one of Sydney's original working-class suburbs, a suburb still wracked by under-employment, drugs and violence. It is territory, however, that, like Redfern and many suburbs before it, is rapidly being bought up and gentrified because of its proximity to the city and relatively cheap housing (though not for much longer). The locals rarely ventured inside the theatre and this is something Company B wanted to change. So this new work met with many of B's targets: it would have a sharp political edge, take an oblique angle to the establishment, be popular and stimulating and offer a new-ish, and certainly appropriate, form of theatrical experience—verbatim theatre.

One potential problem with this play as a piece of theatre was that many people probably knew the story, and even worse, the ending. And they were probably also aware that Souths, though back in competition, had received the wooden spoon and look set to languish at the bottom of the table for a good while longer. Was the experience, therefore, now invalid, upstaged by more recent events?

Unlike a naturalistic play, verbatim theatre neither relies on the joys of an elegantly unfolding plot, nor the Aristotelian unities, but on the timelessness of great characters and the juxtaposition, understatement and blunt honesty of their utterances. We cannot help marvelling at heart-stopping bravery or foolhardy behaviours. The initiating incident a verbatim play seeks to dramatise does need to have some currency, yet it should not feel modish or cynically motivated. Rather it seeks to be a work of oral and performative history. It is about celebrating difficult events of the recent past in an attempt to understand the history of the present, beyond media bias or compression. Reportage can be a treacherous form—no matter the intentions, it can sometimes feel like trading in human misery. Yet idiosyncrasies, intimacy, outrageousness and genuine authenticity make riveting theatrical fare—and storytelling is an art. In developing this play we were hoping to get the balance right between real life and art; the bigger picture and the minutiae; and authenticity and design. As in the finest works of theatre, we wanted to create a work that spoke through the particular to the universal.

There is also something to be said for the deceptive simplicity of the form. Actors play real people who didn't speak their 'lines' to an audience, yet suddenly they now confide in over 300 people. The real people/actors tell us their true stories, yet we must be on the lookout for exaggeration, reticent opacity, maybe nervous obfuscation, or even intentional omissions. What is highlighted and what is suppressed? How much does memory, a new context and time re-shape events to please or offend? What is the relationship between traumas the interviewees once experienced and the relating of this information some time later to a relative stranger? How do real people convey what is important to them? And how do you present this so that it remains dramatically engaging and beyond the quotidian? In many ways verbatim theatre subverts the usual relationship an audience has with a playwright's craft. Authenticity is at once total, and yet perpetually in question.

Company B has a history of successfully presenting verbatim theatre and as far as I understand, is planning on doing more in the future. Recent to the development and production of *Run Rabbit Run* had been The Tectonic Theatre Group's *The Laramie Project* on the death of Matthew Shepard; and ten years earlier had seen Paul Brown's and the Newcastle Workers' Cultural Action Committee's *Aftershocks*. Both of these shows were models for well-constructed, artistically satisfying and well-argued theatre. They were meticulously put together and the words of the people interviewed were never corrupted, simplified or diluted.

For this process (and unlike most verbatim theatre that I know) Alana did all the interviews herself. Indeed she conducted over 30 interviews, mostly at about 70 minutes in duration (though some went as long as two hours). She took about half an hour to get their measure, spent half an hour on more detailed and carefully judged questioning and left about ten minutes to go in for the tough questions. She spoke to some people twice, and, with Mark Courtney, ended up interviewing his wife, children and close mate. These interviews were then transcribed (every interviewee was given a release form to sign) and edited down to what was useful in order to tell the story. Alana did not try to make it a story of goodies and baddies, and looked to Hartigan and Macourt, for example, even Denis Fitzgerald from Parramatta, to give succinct and accurate explanations of their actions. She tried over and again to interview Lachlan Murdoch, but to no avail.

Alana's first contact was Norm Lipson, Souths PR man, and he recommended people to interview. Alana found that each person she spoke to knew ten more people to talk to, who knew ten more, so quickly we had to start drawing lines as to what information, or emotion, or story angle, was needed and what was not. We were looking for stories of dissent, loss, internecine struggles, the main voices of the fightback (like Pappas and Piggins), and those who witnessed, but who may not have played an active part in the struggle—journalists, residents, ex-players and coaches and so on. They may not have marched but nevertheless had things to say about ownership of the club, the game and the country. There were also clear points of concentration for the play: for instance, the way it begins, with stories of where people were when they first heard the news. Information was garnered into what Paul Brown calls 'nodes'. What did they know of the history of the club? What was their perception of the fightback plan, such as it was? How did they feel about the various steps in the legal battle? Alana asked such standard questions alongside those tailored to particular personalities given their relationship to events. Many people felt that the story was both immensely public and deeply personal, so Alana had to tread carefully to win their trust and guarantee transparency of process and accuracy of representation.

We also made a commitment early on, supported entirely by the director Kate Gaul, to the vernacular. All the conversational dead-ends, ellipses and grammatical errors were to stay in the script. This wasn't to mock the speaker, but to reflect accurately what they were saying, and the way they were trying to say it and to give useful grist to the actors. There was never an attempt to mould or finesse the speeches into a more easily digestible form. It was always our intention to maintain characters' dignity and to balance triumphalism with a real depiction of the internal fights and the fact that the chaos is far from over. We did not seek to create villains and heroes—we sought to represent a wide variety of opinions.

We agreed that a broadly chronological approach was the most useful spine for the play and Alana aggregated content in this way. We found that, though the steps in the story were simply jumps in time, they tended to reflect broader thematic concerns of the piece: shock, pride, delusion, foolhardiness and moral courage. Alana gave each section a title in a Brechtian fashion, and the use of these for performance was left up to the production team.

Run Rabbit Run, unlike some works of verbatim theatre perhaps closer to community theatre, was, at least initially, primarily steered by Alana, with comments from Neil and me. The interviewees had the right to alter their testimony and received copies of it in draft form. The option to amend testimony was only taken up by some, mainly for fear of legal repercussions. We had one workshop in the middle of 2003, and the first week or two of rehearsals in December 2003 were spent re-configuring the text. During these processes the input of both the workshop and performance cast, led by director Kate Gaul, was invaluable. Once rehearsals began emails daily flew back and forth between Kate, Alana and I about the play's progress on the floor. Both casts gave crucial insights into the development of the work as a whole, and with respect to their particular characters. The topics discussed, beside the overall story, included cuts (the first read through lasted six hours), the balance between storytelling and dialogue, and how to tighten the focus on fewer characters as the play unfolded. Lacunae were revealed during this time and, as a result, the emotional terrain was mapped and remapped. Alana often had to find new subjects to interview or go back to re-interview previous ones. A huge debt of thanks must go to the production team, and to Neil Armfield, for their good sense and honesty, clear thinking and commitment to telling these stories.

There is no clear way to explain how monumental the task of staging *Run Rabbit Run* was. We all felt beholden, both to the real people and to Alana, to represent the stories offered to us with clarity and fidelity.

Kate made it clear from the outset, though, that the performers were not to mimic the real people, nor feel the pressure to go and meet with the interview subjects themselves. Alana had so much raw material to offer that the amount of work undertaken by all involved was necessarily detailed and all-encompassing. The play was shaped and re-shaped with form and content under constant scrutiny, plus for Kate and the actors there were also the production logistics to consider. We sought to make cuts with integrity, but it was very difficult given the quality of the stories on offer.

Indeed, Alana did an extraordinary job assembling such a cast of rich and diverse voices and her skill made editing very difficult. She was thorough in her preparation and rigorously faithful to her subjects. Her rehearsal draft was persuasive and the process worked simply to distil it. Kate had a very sharp eye for repetition of sentiment or sense and, while acknowledging the cumulative effect of this kind of theatre, was always on the lookout to keep statements succinct and dramatically punchy. Their job was not historical recreation or depiction in the bookish sense, nor a history written by the winners, but a theatrical experience fulfilling the vital function of community storytelling. In constructing the story it was clearly important to ensure it was not all black and white (or red and green), but revealed a level playing field where events and stories could conflict, accumulate and coalesce, leaving us to draw our own conclusions. Of course it also needed to be: a) an accurate distillation of the events, truly representative and scrupulously fair; and b) an engaging piece of theatre.

This was no easy task.

In performance the community seemed to embrace the show. One supporter came with his life-sized rabbit, twice (and paid for two seats both times). Indeed, in performance it often played a bit like a melodrama or a pantomime, with the crowd booing, heckling and cheering. This indicated, as Alana noted, a compelling sense of community ownership. Certainly on opening night there was a roar at the end of the show and many tears as some of the real contributors (Pappas, Courtney and family, Roger, Grasswill, Barb and Marcia) re-lived events close to their hearts.

The show found the balance between inimitable personal experiences and universal significance. *Run Rabbit Run* also offered something quite important for Australian culture: a bridge from sport to art and back again. There was an interesting ritual at work here, something of totemic local relevance—as events were re-examined so they could be absorbed and interpreted anew, even by those who had not been there. We were drawn in to the story and whether we loved footy or not, knew anything about South Sydney or not, we recognised something new and profound in these shared stories of struggle and loss. Here we saw something ineluctably human—a will to power at war with itself; a desire to fight, win and share; and the beauty and all-too-human paradox of people working together, no matter how deluded or deceiving, for the greater good, greater happiness.

Chris Mead
May 2004

Chris Mead is a theatre director. He was Literary Manager of Company B Belvoir St Theatre from 2000–03 and was the Dramaturg on *Run Rabbit Run.*

PLAYWRIGHT'S NOTE

All the words in *Run Rabbit Run* are verbatim from interviews with the people in this story, or from transcripts on the public record—from court transcripts, newspapers and annual reports. This play is a drama which takes what these people said, and how they said it, so capturing the rhythms and music of the Australian vernacular.

It is also very much my version of the events, arranged and edited to elucidate the themes that I think this story evokes and explores. It is not a definitive history of the politics of sport, it is certainly not a definitive history of the politics of the South Sydney Rugby League Club. It was not my priority to write about whether Souths are a good team, whether they deserved to be in the NRL, or even what their struggle says about the corporatisation of sport. It was my ambition to look at the aspects of our Australian nature that the story reveals—the contradictions, the obsessions, the passions and the pain—and to draw from them a story for which the struggle around Souths is simply the lens through which we might view something infinitely more complex and confronting about ourselves.

Neil Armfield, in introducing the 2003 Belvoir season, wrote about 'the complications of empathy: perhaps the most valuable of all human capacities'. It is my hope that this play will make the audience and the reader—passionate sports fans and those who have never been to a Rugby League game in their life (and even secretly detest all sport) alike—empathise with people who may be their most unlikely soul mates ever.

I wish to thank the interviewees—George Piggins, Nicholas Pappas, Mark Courtney, Andrew Denton, Norm Lipson, Jimmy Lahood, Nolene Piggins, Helen Grasswill, Alan Jones, John Hartigan, Robert Corra, Josh Kemp, Eileen McLaughlin, Father Brian Rayner, Roger Harvey, Marcia Seebacher, Barbara Selby, Eric Simms, Denis Fitzgerald, Ian Heads, Anya Courtney, Bronte Courtney, Freya Courtney, Cindy Hawkey, Greg Wilkinson, Robert Taylor, Tasha Lawrence, Peter Macourt and Phillip Pike—for their time and generosity in allowing me to use their words in my play. I must also thank all the copyright holders for their permissions and generosity.

My thanks go to Neil and Rachel and all at Company B for their encouragement and enthusiasm for this project and its premiere season, to everyone who assisted my research, to Chris Mead and Kate Gaul for their incredible work to bring the play to the stage, and to Sharne MacDonald and Vicki Gordon for their consistent genius in Valentine-wrangling. And, finally, thank you to the people of South Sydney, and all the many other places where Souths fans lurk, for enacting a contemporary miracle on Belvoir's doorstep.

Alana Valentine
June 2004

Run Rabbit Run was first produced by Company B at the Belvoir St Theatre, Sydney, on 7 January 2004, with the following cast:

MARK COURTNEY, NORMAN NICHOLAS, PETER MACOURT	Josef Ber
GEORGE PIGGINS, ALAN JONES, ROBERT TAYLOR, JUSTICE FINN, PHILLIP PIKE	Roy Billing
NICHOLAS PAPPAS, DANNY MUNK, ERIC SIMMS, ALAN CATT	Wayne Blair
ANDREW DENTON, ROGER HARVEY, JOHN HARTIGAN, TOM COCKING	Tyler Coppin
BARBARA SELBY, EILEEN McLAUGHLIN, MIKE GIBSON, FREYA COURTNEY	Julie Hamilton
MARCIA SEEBACHER, JOSH KEMP, BRONTE COURTNEY	Jody Kennedy
DENIS FITZGERALD, NORM LIPSON, ALAN JONES, GREG WILKINSON	Russell Kiefel
NOLENE PIGGINS, CAROLINE JONES, RUPERT MURDOCH, P. GERAGHTY	Eliza Logan
HELEN GRASSWILL, CINDY HAWKEY, RUPERT MURDOCH, JEFF COOK, NATASHA (TASHA) LAWRENCE	Georgina Naidu
JIMMY LAHOOD, IAN HEADS, BRIAN RAYNOR, ROBERT CORRA, BARRY MURRAY, ANYA COURTNEY	Alex Sideratos

Director, Kate Gaul
Set Design, Brian Thomson
Costume Design, Genevieve Dugard
Lighting Design, Mark Howett
Sound Design, Jeremy Silver

TIME-LINE

10 October 1999	'Reclaim the Game' downtown Sydney rally draws 40,000 supporters onto the streets in the biggest political sporting rally in history.
15 October 1999	Souths receive news that they have been culled from the Rugby League Premiership after 92 seasons.
8 December 1999	Justice Peter Hely dismisses Souths' application for an injunction for readmission to the 2000 Premiership.
June / July 2000	Souths allege in the Federal Court of Australia that News Limited has contravened the Trade Practices Act and engaged in 'misleading and deceptive conduct'.
August 2000	Kerry Stokes pledges $3 million to South Sydney to satisfy Justice Finn's desire for Souths to prove long-term financial backing.
October 2000	In a 181-page judgement Justice Paul Finn rejects Souths' claims that News Limited has breached the Trade Practices Act.
12 November 2000	80,000 people respond to Finn's decision in an emotional public display of the 'Red and Green Army' and their supporters.
May 2001	Souths appeal to the Full Bench of the Federal Court on the grounds that Justice Finn had 'erred nine times in his November judgement'.
6 July 2001	After almost two years and $2 million in court costs, the Full Bench of the Federal Court vote two to one to support Souths' appeal. Soon after, the NRL invites Souths to rejoin the 2002 competition.

August 2001	News Limited serve Souths with papers, indicating their intention to appeal the Federal Court decision in the High Court of Australia.
December 2001	SSRLFC boast some 20,000 members, a number unprecedented in the history of the game.
March 2002	Souths run onto the field at the SCG in the resurrected Charity Shield match against St George/Illawarra (and retain the shield in a draw) and subsequently begin participation in the 2002 NRL Premiership League.
August 2003	Four of five judges in the High Court overturn the Federal Court ruling that Souths' exclusion from the NRL competition breached the Trade Practices Act. News Limited meet all costs for the hearing.

CHARACTERS

JIMMY LAHOOD, Australian-Lebanese doctor, currently Souths
Board member

GEORGE PIGGINS, ex-South Sydney Rugby League Football Club
Chairman, public face of the fightback campaign

DENIS FITZGERALD, CEO Parramatta Rugby League Football Club
and Leagues Club, public rival of George Piggins

NOLENE PIGGINS, wife of Souths ex-Chairman, George Piggins

DANNY MUNK, CEO Balmain Leagues and Football Club

JOSH KEMP, 25-year-old factory worker, co-ordinates Souths fan
and volunteer clubs

NICHOLAS PAPPAS, Australian-Greek solicitor, now Souths RLFC
Chairman

ANDREW DENTON, television and radio personality

NORM LIPSON, feisty Australian-Jewish journalist, ex-Media
Manager at Souths

ALAN JONES, radio broadcaster and former Souths Football Club
Manager

IAN HEADS, journalist and author, resigned over *Telegraph*
treatment of Souths

ROGER HARVEY, Souths supporter, blind

MARK COURTNEY, Souths supporter, author of *Moving the
Goalposts*

MARCIA SEEBACHER, supporter who organised merchandise during
the fightback

BARBARA SELBY, Marcia's mother, also organised merchandise

NORMAN NICHOLAS, Souths supporter

ERIC SIMMS, former Souths player (1965–75), indigenous heritage

NATASHA (TASHA) LAWRENCE, ex-Leagues Club employee,
indigenous heritage

JOHN HARTIGAN, CEO of News Limited

PHILLIP PIKE, Souths fan and volunteer

MIKE GIBSON, *Telegraph* columnist

HELEN GRASSWILL, ABC *Australian Story* television journalist

PETER MACOURT, Chief Operating Officer, News Limited

RUPERT MURDOCH, Chairman and Chief Executive, News Corporation

EILEEN McLAUGHLIN, salt-of-the-earth Australian-Irish volunteer

FATHER BRYAN RAYNER, Catholic priest, Maroubra parish

TOM COCKING, Souths Leagues Club Manager

JUSTICE PAUL FINN, judge of Federal Court

ALAN CATT, letter writer

P. GERAGHTY, letter writer

JEFF COOK, letter writer

BARRY MURRAY, Souths fan

CINDY HAWKEY, wife of Mark, mother of Anya, Bronte and Freya

ANYA COURTNEY, aged 11, daughter of Mark and Cindy

BRONTE COURTNEY, aged 9, daughter of Mark and Cindy

FREYA COURTNEY, aged 7, daughter of Mark and Cindy

GREG WILKINSON, Souths fan, friend of Mark Courtney

CAROLINE JONES, television presenter and author

ROBERT TAYLOR, Juniors referee, indigenous heritage

ROBERT CORRA, 2SER-FM *View from the Hill* broadcaster

PLAYER, can be played by any member of the cast

Interval may be taken at the end of Act Two Scene Three.

ACT ONE

ONE: ELIMINATION

JIMMY LAHOOD: I was on my way here. I got in the lift. I went up the lift to meet George. The lift doors opened. George was walking back to the lift to come down and tell everyone else and he looked at me.

GEORGE PIGGINS: The bastards have shot us out, Jimmy.

JIMMY: That's when I found out.

PLAYER: Dr Jimmy Lahood.

JIMMY: I was in disbelief. George and I had thought all along when push came to shove they wouldn't take on such a powerful public sentiment against it. But George just looked at me and his look sort of said, 'Shit. The war's begun.'

DENIS FITZGERALD: Tradition doesn't turn a balance sheet from red to black.

PLAYER: Denis Fitzgerald.

DENIS: Souths fans kept hammering the tradition and past success of the club, but a line was drawn in the sand in December 1997 and the only tradition was the same for all clubs—that was, the last two years of competition.

NOLENE PIGGINS: I was at home.

PLAYER: Nolene Piggins.

NOLENE: I was expecting that news, but when I actually heard it… probably there's always a little bit of hope… you know what's going to be, but then you're hoping that it won't be. So it was very sad… I felt very empty.

DANNY MUNK: It's a pity Souths don't realise change is necessary.

PLAYER: Danny Munk.

DANNY: They will die a lingering death.

JOSH KEMP: I was expecting the worst, y'know, everyone was.

PLAYER: Josh Kemp.

JOSH: I was working afternoon shift at the factory and I received a call from a friend. A few people at work took the opportunity to rub it in and I weren't in the best of moods. As can be expected. I didn't finish work until eleven o'clock that night so I had to quickly get changed and go into the Leagues Club and, by that time, the spirit of everyone had turned around and everyone was, all of a sudden, over their disappointment and willing to fight, and didn't care that we were kicked out. Like, they had this belief... 'No, we're not going to be beaten.' I was still down on myself because I hadn't been around everyone... I'd been at work just thinking of all the worst things, but then when I got to the club and seeing everyone like that, I felt a sense of strongness about it. I'd describe it—the spirit of South Sydney was with me.

NICHOLAS PAPPAS: I had a phone call from a very close friend that I used to go to all the Souths games with when we were young.

PLAYER: Nicholas Pappas.

NICHOLAS: It was the same guy who called me the day John Lennon died because that was our other love, the Beatles and sixties music generally and Souths, and the two went very much hand in hand, because it was a peak in music and the peak for Souths. The two worst pieces of news someone could tell me and it was the same person who rang me.

It was terrible. And it was not so much a Rugby League thing. It was your childhood, it was your old Greek grandmother who knew nothing about football, dressed in her black, asking every Sunday, 'Did Souths win?', in Greek. She'd never watched a football game in her life, but it was part of the family. Growing up in these suburbs over here. It was part of our upbringing. We knew we were up against the wall. We knew the firing squad was aiming at us, but we thought the letter would come at the last second. It's that feeling like when someone is on death row, you can't actually believe they're going to get executed, and when it happens there's just this dull thud.

ANDREW DENTON: When I got to the club, it was a bit like—I hesitate to use this word in these times—it was a bit like a war zone.

PLAYER: Andrew Denton.

ANDREW: The best way I could describe it, it was like a really civilised lynch mob. These were the people that would have lynched Rupert Murdoch, except they would have known in the end—they would have been too decent to do it.

NORM LIPSON: I was right outside this club.

PLAYER: Norm Lipson.

NORM: It was a sunny Friday afternoon and we knew the National Rugby League was meeting at the time to work out their phoney criteria which was tailored specifically to get rid of Souths. I remember the crowd going 'Boo', 'No', and the tears started flowing. I can remember Ray Hadley went to air breathlessly announcing it and he sounded quite happy and gloating about it and then I can remember the groundswell of emotion, people screaming as if they'd lost a member of their own family. And they had. They'd lost a tradition, a family tradition.

ALAN JONES: I was most probably at the radio station at 2UE.

PLAYER: Alan Jones.

ALAN: I can't remember that. I suppose mentally I knew they'd been culled anyway. They never had a chance. It was a corrupt process.

ROGER HARVEY: Excluded from the competition? Well, I was—I was—I was here, at Lewisham Hospital, I live here because I'm blind.

PLAYER: Roger Harvey.

ROGER: I heard it on the radio. Ah… the supporters take me to the game. I've got the radio—and it tells me… ah… what goes on. I like the sounds of everyone shouting. That's right. Yes. I shout myself. Yeah, yeah. Have a good time. Yeah.

MARK COURTNEY: I was en route from work to the club.

PLAYER: Mark Courtney.

MARK: It was weird really. It, it—it felt like a bit of a punch in the stomach. It was a physical reaction… um, I actually had to park—had to stop the car because I actually felt for a moment as—a bit nauseous, it was quite weird. Um… and I—I decided that it was—you know, you prepare yourself for things—I think and I think I—and you prepare yourself for things to happen at a certain time, you know, and I think that… um… [pause] I'd prepared myself for it to occur at twelve-thirty or whatever the exact time was, and in fact what had happened was the League had rung George Piggins at the club and told him beforehand that this was going to occur and Souths—and George went straight down to the auditorium and had already announced it.

So before the—it might have been two-thirty I think, two-thirty p.m. was the announcement, two o'clock was the—and it was on the two o'clock news. So I was going to be there by about quarter past two… ah, and at—on the two o'clock news on whatever station they were talking about… ah, you know, fans were starting to gather at the South Sydney Leagues Club in preparation for an announcement… ah, and then they finished the news and then they had the weather or whatever and then they had a live cross. They were just going to cross live back to the South Sydney Leagues Club now… ah, and they had a reporter there who said that George Piggins had just announced to the crowd that Souths had been excluded. I just—I just felt sick.

It was like, you know, you prepare yourself for something to happen at a certain time, and I'd just—and I wasn't ready, I—if it had been two-thirty, I would have been ready somehow, but I wasn't ready. Even that—I'd been preparing for it for months and that twenty-five minutes stuffed me up completely and I actually—I felt sick and it was—it was a—it was the most weird feeling, it was like, I stopped the car, I got out of the car, and it felt like every car was going in slow motion and people were looking at me as though, you know, what's that—as though I'd—it—as though everyone could see what was happening to me, which of course wasn't true, and after a couple of minutes I got back in and went to the club.

People were, you know, walking around swearing and yelling and one guy was burning a Fox Sports logo thing and people were crying and, you know, it was weird. I stopped just at the—at the park there, there were some girl sitting there, she was about, I don't know, twenty-five, with a Souths jumper on, and she was just sitting there with her head in her hands crying, and I stopped and just talked to her and, and, you know, I was—I said to her, 'Don't worry,' you know, 'Don't worry, we'll beat them, we'll beat them'. And I had no idea what, what, you know, what the machinations were going to be, but I just had this view that they couldn't get away with it, they just couldn't get away with it, you know, and I was talking to this girl saying, 'Don't worry, don't worry, we'll beat them', and I was really calm then.

And then as I was walking across the road, I started crying as well. I was—I remember signing the book, and I looked up and saw the [*indicating the rabbit emblem*] —and I—it was the tears just came.

DENIS FITZGERALD: Rugby League is definitely a business.

PLAYER: Denis Fitzgerald.

DENIS: There's just—sure it's a sport, but so many sports are big business, if you look at tennis and golf and British soccer and American football, basketball. I mean, oh, you just can't—cannot run anything on emotion... um, and at the end of the day it's usually the stronger or strongest financial teams or entities, companies, that—that—that still survive and so you just—you just can't have a competition based on emotion.

TWO: GLORY DAYS

BARBARA SELBY: Okay, um... I came to live in Redfern when I was two.

PLAYER: Barbara Selby.

BARBARA: My mum always said one of our first words was 'Rabbitohs', because of the rabbitoh man coming around the street.

PLAYER: Volunteer and Souths fan.

BARBARA: Mum used to buy the rabbits [*with a laugh*] —we'd have them braised or roasted and, you know, I mean, you acquired the taste for it— [*with a laugh*] and as I grew up, my dad used to say to me, 'Oh, come on, love, let's go and watch the big boys play'. We'd sit over at Redfern Oval and watch the game, and I'm sixty-seven now, so I've been around Redfern and Souths a long time.

NORMAN NICHOLAS: South Sydney was a foundation club in 1908.

PLAYER: Norman Nicholas.

NORMAN: And it's not an institution, it's a way of life.

JIMMY LAHOOD: We contributed more to Rugby League than anyone else.

PLAYER: Dr Jimmy Lahood. Board Member.

JIMMY: We contributed financially, we contributed more legends, more great players, more people who represented Australia in Rugby League. We had people working every weekend for ninety-two years coaching kids to play Rugby League. All that goodwill that Souths has fostered for the game, you can't say to us, 'Get away, you don't own any part of this game'.

NORM LIPSON: This area is full of fighters.

PLAYER: Norm Lipson.

NORM: They were unionists—they had to fight the bosses on the wharves.

PLAYER: Former Souths Media Manager.

NORM: Jimmy's cousin Peter said it, 'They picked the wrong team'. These people are used to fighting for every scrap that they've got. Every scrap of food they've got. They're used to fighting for every meagre possession they have. Pardon my expression, I don't know if I'm allowed to swear in front of you, but the general attitude was, 'You're

From left: Josef Ber as Norman Nicholas, Russell Kiefel as Norm Lipson, Julie Hamilton as Barbara Selby and Jody Kennedy as Marcia Seebacher in the 2004 Company B production. (Photo: Heidrun Löhr)

not fucking taking my football team, brother. Just try it.' It'd be like trying to take my wife away, or my kid.

JIMMY LAHOOD: I was born in Redfern. My dad went to school at Cleveland Street High. My family has been in Redfern since the 1890s and we'd all been attached to this football club.

A reporter in the *Herald*, Steve Mascord, had a bit of a shot at us. He called us Gucci-wearing South Sydney supporters. I might wear Gucci and other labels, yeah I wear good clobber. But my dad was in the rag trade. But the difference was that we all started as battlers. When we were marching I was carrying a CFMEU flag and one of the Souths supporters said to me, 'You're a doctor, what are you carrying that for?', and I said, 'Listen, my blood line is all working-class. I was born working-class and I'll die working-class and my profession doesn't change that.'

NORMAN NICHOLAS: They showed it on the TV… they showed some of our supporters who were handicapped or disabled…

NORM: They wanted to make out we were halfwits.

JIMMY: The majority of our players, in the first team ever, earned their living selling rabbits. And people would say, 'Let's go and watch the Rabbitohs playing footy'. And that's where the name came from. The Red and Green is because they were all Irish Catholics who formed this club. They used the Cardinal Red of their faith and the Myrtle Green of their homeland. That is the history of this club. And now I'm an Arab, [*indicating others*] he's a Jew and he's Greek.

PLAYER: Marcia and Barbara.

MARCIA SEEBACHER: Oh, my first memory, was probably—I mean, I remember going to the games, but my first big memory was, like, in the '70 Grand Final.

PLAYER: Marcia Seebacher.

MARCIA: It was the first Grand Final I was allowed to go to, and everyone used to sleep out at the Cricket Ground to get—to be the first there, and I was never allowed to sleep out, but I remember going to the '70 Grand Final because I was old enough, and I think I was nine or something. I remember sitting on the—on the Hill area, the cheap seats. We'd get the train in from Panania, the whole family—

BARBARA SELBY: No, Greenacre.

MARCIA: I remember it from Panania.

BARBARA: I didn't go to football for a while when I had these five children, but then... um, my son, after the '67 Grand Final, we watched it on TV, and he said, 'Oh Mum, we've got to go, we've got to go'. So the next year I started taking him and then... um, he... um... [*pause*] it was at Newtown Oval. We went to Henson Park, him and I, and... um, he said, 'Oh, Mum, can I jump the fence, can I jump the fence?', and he was a very tiny little, like he was only a little, he was about eight, and... um, but he was tiny for his age, and so I said, 'Oh okay, off you go'. So he jumped the fence and he's running out on the field and slap bang into Johnny Sattler's legs, and Sats put his hand on his head and stood and talked to him for five minutes, and he come back and he was like ten foot tall. 'Mum, we've got to wait, we've got to wait, Johnny Sattler wants to meet you', and I said, 'Johnny Sattler wants to meet me?'. And he said, 'Yes'. So we went round to near the dressing sheds and... um, out comes Johnny Sattler, so Robert introduced me to Johnny Sattler and from then on... um, every time we saw Johnny Sattler he remembered us. He's got an amazing memory, absolutely amazing—and we were at the Grand Final when Sats got his jaw broken, weren't we?

MARCIA: Yes.

BARBARA: As soon you saw him you knew that there was something bad wrong, you know. It was very inspiring, but, I mean, you cringed with every—every time you saw him tackled, you cringed because you knew that it must be hurting.

> *Both laugh in amazement.*

ANDREW DENTON: Okay, when Souths went bankrupt in the early '70s, I think it was '71, Souths were playing Newtown at Newtown, at Henson Park.

PLAYER: Andrew Denton. Broadcaster.

ANDREW: It was a rainy day, the dressing rooms were crap and there was water pouring in and the Souths players were warming up and the Souths secretary, a bit of a wide boy call Charlie Gibson, came in and said, 'Boys, I've got bad news, the club's gone bust, don't know if we can pay you, have a good game'. And out he walked, and there was a stunned silence, as you might imagine. And Clive Churchill, the legendary Clive Churchill, Souths coach, looked around and then said, 'Well, that's enough of the fancy warm-up speeches, let's have a game'.

MARK COURTNEY: I started right at the end of the golden era.

PLAYER: Mark Courtney. Souths fan.

MARK: 1969 they lost the Grand Final, well that was pretty tragic, but it was an aberration as far as I was concerned. And then the year—the next year they won the Grand Final and the year after that they won the Grand Final, so my first three years, which was, you know, the time I was eight, nine and ten, I formed all my impressions about football at that time.

And when they lost the Semi Final in 1972 and didn't make the Grand Final, it was as though someone had actually come to me and said, you know, Santa Claus isn't real, you know.

So after that there was this big decline into—into the '70s, they came last in '75, and made the semis in '80 and '84, just, and then there was a brief flicker of goldenness in the late '80s, so they were a good side, from '86 through '89, they were a very good side— 1989 was an excellent season and then 1990 they finished last and that was the—you know, 1990 was the start of it all really, the start of the—the—well, it wasn't—can't go worst than last, I suppose, but '90 through '93 they were dreadful, dreadful, and, you know, last, third last, second last, or something, you know, down in the bottom three. '94 they showed some promise and then '95 they went down again. '95, '96, '97, '98 they were awful, and then '99 they were quite good with the promise of building. So they had had a lot of ordinary times, but you still had great wins in those bad years, you know. You had days that you remember.

ANDREW DENTON: I started supporting Souths when I was eight.

PLAYER: Andrew Denton.

ANDREW: I was given a pair of Souths football socks when I was ten and I was a really small kid, and they came up to about my... ah, chest, but I—every time I wore them I thought I was Bob McCarthy and I still have them. They're the oldest living piece of clothing I have and... ah... um... my mum always used to complain, saying, you know, 'You're not doing your school work because all you're dreaming about is being half-back for South Sydney', and I never had the heart to tell her she was right.

He laughs. Pause.

I think... ah... I think Rugby League is the—is the toughest, without question, the toughest football code in the world. Rugby League is to rugby the way boxing is to wrestling, in that wrestling actually requires enormous athletic skills and it's an incredibly entertaining thing, but everyone knows that boxing is the real deal. The same as Rugby League. It's gladiatorial, and when you go and watch it and you sit there and see what those players are absorbing, it's—it is primal and utterly compelling and that's—that's—it does it for me every time.

ERIC SIMMS: Yeah... ah, gees, what did I play? Yes, I played '65 Grand Final against the great St George, we lost, of course, 12–8.

PLAYER: Eric Simms.

ERIC: Then we played '67, we won the first competition in '67, '68, lost '69, won '70, won '71.

PLAYER: Souths legend.

ERIC: I work on the waterfront now. I've been doing the waterfront for going on twenty-four years.

PLAYER: Career points: 1,841. Which is the top points scored by any Souths player. Ever. 23 tries, 803 goals, 86 field goals.

ERIC: Well, in my era, see, it was great, it was enormous as a matter of fact, because being Aboriginal too and them coming up through—through the junior grades and that, and making it to the big time, it was—it was tremendous, and playing with the likes of the players that I was associated with at that time, yeah, it was a golden era.

PLAYER: Averages show that every time Eric Simms walked onto the field for Souths in his eleven seasons he was worth 8.9 points per game.

ERIC: When a goal kick come up I just hope and prayed that it would go between the posts and, of course, yes, a lot of times it was luck, but I practised a lot at the time, you know, so it did become a natural thing, so yes, that responsibility was on me all the time, but, you know, it didn't seem to worry me any, I just took it in me stride and as I said, hoped for the best.

MARK COURTNEY: My wife Cindy and I were—moved in together…

PLAYER: Mark Courtney.

MARK: … and then came the biggest—the biggest conflict, which was that… um, we got offers to work in America for a year and Cindy—it had always been one of Cindy's goals, unstated but nevertheless one of her goals, unstated to me. Because you don't state every goal when you start—you know, when you start a relationship, but this came up pretty quickly that, you know, it was always one of her stated goals to, to live and work overseas, and it had always been one of my goals to not do that… [*with a laugh*] and so a huge conflict ensued that took about a year of our relationship to sort out and, you know, we had lots of arguments and discussions in this about everything, and in the end I had to—I had to face the inescapable fact which was that no matter what I said about loving going to the beach, and loving the Australian climate and missing my friends and wanting to listen to Roy and HG and wanting to see… plays… Midnight Oil and blah, blah, blah, the inescapable truth was that the real reason I didn't want to go overseas was I'd have to miss too many Souths games and take a year out of—of that continuum, both with Greg and with Souths, and I just—I couldn't—I just said—and—and, it was a big—it was a big, big crossroad for me, you know, at the time. I was twenty-six and it was a big bloody crossroad, and I had to decide—well, between us, Cindy and I had to decide what to do and… um, we came to some sort of a compromise which meant that we would stay at home for another year and if she was still as determined to do it, then I would do it.

And through the fate of it all, about eight months later Qantas announced that they were going to post people overseas in my particular area to England, to America and Singapore, and I got the job in England and so I managed to live there for two years without leaving my job, but still had to leave Souths and Greg for two years and it was… [*pause*] a big growth experience in my life, because I realised that in fact it was okay to do that. But it was… [*pause*] hard—I don't have that link with anybody else in my life and—I met him at the football. [*He laughs.*] I met him on the Hill in 1977. We just happened to bump into each other a couple more times and then started to sit together and still do.

TASHA LAWRENCE: I worked at the Souths Leagues Club.

PLAYER: Natasha Lawrence.

TASHA: I just love watchin' 'em... the men mainly... y'know... [*laughing*] the men... oh, yeah... yeah, yeah... I love aggressive games... I love screamin' and shoutin' for my team... so...

NOLENE PIGGINS: Well... [*pause*] Souths has always been my football team.

PLAYER: Nolene Piggins.

NOLENE: I was born and bred in Alexandria. I went through school with George, but I didn't follow South Sydney because of George. George had nothing to do with Souths being my football team. A lot of people think—because I married George... um, so—that was my father's and my uncle's and my family's football team. I—I'm— I—I like everything that I—that—that—everything that's—that I've had in my life, I treasure that. I wouldn't change it. And that's what Souths means to me. Souths means that that's—you know, I wouldn't like someone to—to take my child. I mean, I can't lose a child and replace that. I mean... [*pause*] they thought that South Sydney people would just follow Eastern Suburbs, because they... [*pause*] you know, they had money and that—that was close on our boundaries and—and so go and follow another team or merge with a club and follow a merged club. I mean—

But you can't. Because they—because—because—you know, once you lose something, it's gone. I'm just saying, once something dies, it's gone. I don't lose a—I lost my father, I can't just say to somebody—call somebody else Dad.

Like—why were we the targeted club? Why were we the only club that Super League didn't speak to? To ask us to go and play in another competition? How did—well—well, that's—that's—that's what made it so—so—so—that's what hurt us so much.

THREE: THE LEAGUE OF SUPERMEN

IAN HEADS: Right from when the game began in 1908, Rugby League had been under the control of the Australian Rugby League, the body which effectively ran the competition for the teams.

PLAYER: Ian Heads. Journalist and Rugby League historian.

Eliza Logan as Nolene Piggins in the 2004 Company B production.
(Photo: Heidrun Löhr)

IAN: During 1994, when the battle lines for pay TV dominance in Australia were being drawn, the Brisbane Bronco's sold the idea of a 'Super League' to News Limited. You want subscribers, give them the cream of the League. Lose the duds. Skim off the best and people will pay to watch it on TV. Pay TV.

ALAN JONES: The Super League was going to take the game to the world.

PLAYER: Alan Jones. General Manager of Souths in 1994.

ALAN: And they thought it was the equivalent of World Series Cricket and they were going to have all this hoopla and fandango and dancing girls and so on.

GEORGE PIGGINS: I remember very well the February 1995 meeting where News Limited and Ken Cowley presented the Super League blueprint to the clubs.

PLAYER: George Piggins.

GEORGE: I asked Smith, David Smith from News Limited, which of the clubs would be in the Super League. He says to me, 'I can assure you, I won't be speaking to you'. News didn't want to talk to the so-called 'brokes' like us and Wests.

IAN HEADS: The plan was for twelve licensed, privately-owned Super League clubs.

GEORGE: We were asked to sign a loyalty agreement to the ARL. Which we did. To me, the whole thing was unbelievable. Here were Murdoch and Co walking in off the street, you know what I mean, and taking over football. I was filthy. That was when Bullfrog Moore, at Canterbury, put a broom up the arse of the ARL and jumped to Super League. Until they signed, the breakaway Super League had only newcomers and blow-ins. But they were offering truck-loads of money to the players. It was every club, and every man for himself. And soon the clubs and players were jumping like salmon swimming upstream.

IAN: In 1996, the Federal Court decides the Super League can run their competition in 1997. The ARL runs a separate competition.

GEORGE: I honestly believe that if the ARL clubs had stuck together and toughed out one more season, in 1998, that Super League would have fallen on its face. Despite all the hype, Super League had had one poor and unconvincing season and vast amounts of money had been poured into that black hole.

IAN: December 19, 1997, there was the first talk of sticky-taping the two competitions back together and reducing the number of teams from the twenty-two that were playing in both comps, to fourteen. Eight teams were not going to make the cut. Not going to be allowed to play. And the ARL agreed to this. Agreed to cut teams that had been loyal to its competition.

GEORGE: I wasn't going to be invited to be part of any board or committee that might run the thing. I wasn't wanted and Souths weren't wanted.

IAN: Neil Whittaker is the CEO of the ARL and Ian Frykberg is the head honcho of Super League. And they enter into an agreement to form a joint board. The ARL would join with Super League and become the National Rugby League and form a joint competition. A reduced competition.

ALAN JONES: Neil Whittaker's come in.

PLAYER: Alan Jones.

ALAN: He's under siege, he doesn't know what to do, and of course they're all seduced by money and being flown around in jets, and Rupert's people, not Rupert Murdoch, Rupert's people, duchessing, and they can't resist any of that. But it reached the point, and this is often forgotten, where the ARL retained their strength with the public and the other mob had plenty of money but no, no public support.

So they needed us more than we needed them and that was the greatest fallacy in all of this, Whittaker sold out. Once you sell out the economic control of the game you sell out everything. So then Super League had a majority on the amalgamated Board, they had control of the finance and all the rest of it, so then what happens? They start concocting the criteria to decide who'll be in. Where did fourteen teams come from? Why was that the magic number? There's no rationale for it, nothing. Just plucked out of the sky.

FOUR: THE ACID TEST

JOHN HARTIGAN: I can't talk about the actual criteria being flawed.

PLAYER: John Hartigan. CEO, News Limited.

JOHN: But I can talk about the fact that Souths weren't targeted. The equity that News Limited had in the criteria and the whole decision making was equally shared with the ARL. It's constantly seen as News doing this and News doing that... the reality is that we had a partner in this venture and they supported the same views. So I would strongly defend that Souths weren't targeted.

TELEGRAPH: The clubs were assessed at two levels.

PLAYER: As reported in the *Daily Telegraph*.

TELEGRAPH: The first level, called the basic criteria, examined playing facilities, administration, solvency and development. The second level, called the selection criteria, rated the clubs on crowd support, competition results, sponsorship and finances. The exceptions to the overall process were Brisbane, New Zealand and Auckland. The rules included that any club which merged before the deadline would not be included in the criteria scoring.

JOHN: I might even go one step further. If you look at the audience and what News represents, particularly in this city, it is that urban grittiness that Souths proudly reflect. And this is not just measured comment with hindsight, but the reality is that they reflect broadly the audience of many of our commercial businesses. I can't see why we would target those people for that reason.

GEORGE PIGGINS: We weren't targeted?

PLAYER: George Piggins.

GEORGE: We weren't targeted, well, what's that—? [*He laughs.*] Mate, I can laugh at that one. We were targeted for this reason, that we were poor. Like, what I mean, like, we were, you know, we were really scrambling to meet the criteria even though we did meet it. If we merged with Easts, if we did what we was told, we could stay. Well, we didn't want to merge and we didn't do what we was told. And so they got the knives out.

I just think that football isn't business, it's sport, and at the end of the day you're trying to provide a product for your community, and if you break square, you've done a wonderful job... [*pause*] if you got yourself into a little bit of debt, well, you've only got to adjust your budgets for next year, as long as you can get an overdraft to carry you through, but if you got into financial trouble big time, you're probably going to disappear.

DENIS FITZGERALD: Just like General George Piggins, Custer took one division of two hundred and twenty-five men straight up the middle of the valley and they were all massacred.

PLAYER: Denis Fitzgerald. CEO, Parramatta Eels.

DENIS: I would welcome George to be alongside me in the trenches. But I'd be very worried if General George was also the scout and chief strategist of my division.

GEORGE: You reckon I was hard, tough and uncompromising as a footballer. I can't say the same about you. As a footballer I don't have any stand-out memories of you.

DENIS: We can't afford to lose more ground and marketability through continuing off-field dramas and endless and costly court cases.

GEORGE: I remember a bloke once saying to me about the treachery surrounding the whole Rugby League battle, 'George, the more I understand humans, the better I love my dog'. Denis, every time I see your name I have this terrible urge to walk my dogs.

DENIS: Oh, look, based—based on the criteria, I thought the criteria was fair. It was independently assessed by Ernst and Young I think were the—the… um, auditors. Ah, I—I—I had no qualms about the fairness of it.

JIMMY LAHOOD: The NRL sent us a fax telling us that they had not accepted the Juniors sponsorship as a sponsorship. They were saying it was a grant, 1.5 million a year 'til 2002, was a grant. And you got double the points for sponsorships as you did for grants. So we lost a lot of points. And juniors development, like, the littlees, wasn't even counted in the criteria. So in the end, when they published the criteria ranking results, we were ranked seventeenth. Behind Norths, behind Wests, bottom of the table. Seventeenth. And they only wanted fourteen teams.

GEORGE: I've just had a phone call from Neil Whittaker. They've shot us out.

◆ ◆ ◆

FIVE: THE PLAN

MARK COURTNEY: There was no fightback plan.

PLAYER: Mark Courtney.

MARK: At about five or six or something, I don't know what time it was, some time late in the afternoon, the Board came down and read a resolution that, you know, we—the Board of the South Sydney Football Club—reject, rejects totally the decision, rejects the implication of fairness and will not abide, you know, will, will— we'll be fighting this decision in the courts, and that's all they— that's all everyone wanted to hear, you know, because that's what they'd been saying for months. And now, it was—you know—I made a speech myself, it was about seven o'clock, but I just—I felt that I just had to—I just got up, and I said, you know, that—I likened it to—to the referee blowing the whistle at the scrum. In the old days, when scrums were really scrums, the two packs used to stand there and sort of eye each other off and it was pretty—you know, when the scrum packed down it was a vicious packing of fallen, like, antelopes almost, and I—I said, you know, all that's happened today is the referee has blown his whistle to pack down. And as far as I'm concerned, all I say is, 'Let's fuckin' well pack down'. And there was just this huge roar.

PHIL PIKE: You seen all these people who you never knew.

PLAYER: Phil Pike. Pikey.

PHIL: You never knew 'em. You just seen 'em at the football and said, 'G'day, how ya goin'?' 'Aw, Jesus Christ, what happened to the forwards? They just didn't work. Mate, they done nothin'.' 'Mate, what about? Oh. What about the two kicks over here?'… That's it. That's all ya ever said. You didn't know their name. Didn't know nothin' about 'em. You didn't know where they worked. An' suddenly, the next minute all these people… An' suddenly, the next minute when George said we're gonna do this. That's it, bang. Everyone just went, 'Okay. Righto.'

ANDREW DENTON: Look, for me it was a—a fortunate or unfortunate confluence of things about which I felt really passionate.

PLAYER: Andrew Denton.

ANDREW: It was my football team that I'd loved since I was a kid, but that wasn't enough. It was about... ah, media power in this country. A subject about which I feel very passionate, but that wasn't enough. It happened to be both those things plus such a glaring injustice, and such a classic example of the big end of town walking over the small end of town, that the three together, it was like... ah, for me it was... um—an unarguable mixture, it just couldn't be—I knew that if I didn't respond however I could, that I—for the rest of my life I would feel that I'd done the wrong thing. It required an answer and there are many, many causes that call people and it may not have been the most noble, but it just happened to be those three things, all of which I felt very passionately about, mixed into one. It was one of those fabulous times where it didn't matter the consequences, it was just so transparently appropriate to fight until there was—because it was the point of principle.

Tyler Coppin as Andrew Denton and Alex Sideratos (behind) as Dr Jimmy Lahood in the 2004 Company B production. (Photo: Heidrun Löhr)

I spoke with my wife about it a few times and I discussed the fact that, you know, News was an organisation that worked around the world and, you know, I sometimes did work in England and that, you know, you just don't know where that leads to. I certainly knew that, you know, there was a cost here in Sydney straightaway. I remember talking to a friend of mine who was a senior sports journalist actually, and he just said, 'Look, I respect what you're doing, but it's a waste of time, you can't win it', and a lot of my friends were just really puzzled and some—some people thought I was doing it for the publicity, like wow, yeah, quite the opposite effect for me. Look, I knew it was not a great thing for my career, but it's—you can't do everything based on what's in it for me. I mean, you can't.

MIKE GIBSON: It was one of the most violent dust-ups that I ever saw in Rugby League.

PLAYER: Mike Gibson.

MIKE: The Saturday afternoon in 1973 at the SCG, when George Piggins took on Malcolm Reilly. They brawled like a pair of Kilkenny cats, up and down the sideline, in front of the old members' stand. George, the hard as nails little hooker for the South Sydney Rabbitohs, Malcolm the Pom, the fearless lock forward for Manly. And after they had finally dragged them apart, when they appeared before the judiciary that Monday night, George muttered in my ear.

GEORGE: Tell you what, Gibbo, if I could have got my finger behind his eyeball, I'd have ripped it out.

MIKE: Today, the best part of thirty years later, George exhibits the same kind of toe-to-toe toughness, as he vows to go down with the ship, rather than see it lost to the enemy. South Sydney has to face the reality that it's no longer the force that it used to be. And if the game of Rugby League is to survive it has to pay its way and move with the times.

HELEN GRASSWILL: It seemed that News Limited had made up their mind and because of that they couldn't see.

PLAYER: Helen Grasswill. Television journalist.

HELEN: On one level they'd been badly advised and on another level the situation was more complex than anybody really knew. Some of their advisers were doing, I think, what they really believed was right. It's just that they didn't understand the complexity of what they were dealing with in this football club. Red and Green is Christmas. And the Rabbit is Easter and I think that right from an early age, Souths people are hooked in in a way that I don't think they are with other clubs because I just think that there's something... which might sound mad... but I think there's something as base as that which pervades our society, our Christian-based society, and Souths embodies it and somehow brings together all those mythologies. Andrew Denton puts it as the Anzac tradition... you think that it doesn't really exist, but it does in South Sydney, and I think that is what they missed.

I was talking with someone very high up in News Limited, and it was just a casual conversation, and I said something to the effect of what impressed me about Souths was the way they looked after their community, and the comment that came back to me was, 'Oh well, Rupert will buy the place and make it a community centre', and I just thought, this whole organisation just doesn't get it. It may have been made as a joke.

PLAYER: Norm Lipson and Jimmy Lahood.

NORM: I said to my son, 'Mate, we're going to fight and we're going to come back'. I promised him that. I had no right to promise him that. But I had the right to promise him we were going to fight.

JIMMY: It's more than Souths now. I've got to teach my kids something. I'll never forget that my father probably loved Souths more than any other human being I've known over my lifetime, and he said to me, 'Son, you're not going to beat this guy. You can't beat this guy.'

NORM: My dad said the same, and he's a very intelligent guy.

JIMMY: 'I'm telling you,' my dad said, 'Souths are finished. And the game's dead too. Souths will die and the game will die with it. But you won't beat these people. They're unbeatable. And you guys are going to get bashed up and you're going to get hurt and the pain you feel today is only going to be multiplied every time they bash you.' And I looked at him, and my kids were sitting around the dinner table, and I said to him, 'It's not how you brought me up. You told me if someone stepped on my toes to step on their neck.' It's an old

Arabic proverb. He said to me, 'But you can't beat him. The odds are incredible.' And I said, 'That's not what you taught me. You taught me that if I was in the right, not to back down for anyone. We're in the right, we're not going to back down.' And he said, 'You can't beat 'em in the courts, they'll find a million ways to beat you'. And I said, 'It don't matter. It don't matter what they do to us or where they lead us, we'll find our own way back. And it doesn't matter if we're going down, we'll keep shooting as we're going down, and if we hurt them, or if we scratch them, that'll do it.' Norm used to say, 'An ant is small, but if you get enough ants in a bed, they'll drive a man crazy'. And that's what we did. We were driving them out of their heads. They didn't want to hear about us in the finish.

NORM: If you think one individual can't make a difference, you've never been to bed with a mozzie flying around.

END OF ACT ONE

ACT TWO

ONE: THE COWBOY SOLICITOR

NICHOLAS PAPPAS: I went to a function at the Opera House.

PLAYER: Nicholas Pappas.

NICHOLAS: I'd never been to a Souths function in my life. Even though I'd been to every game, I'd never go back to the club to meet the players or anything. It was always straight home to watch the replay on TV. I was asked by an accountant to go to a fundraiser at the Bennelong. At the end we all had to leave our business cards on the table. And as George walked past, the guy next to me said, 'Go on, ask him now. Tell him you're a lawyer.' I said, 'G'day, George'. I was nervous, he was another hero from my past, and I said, 'Listen, if you need any legal advice, I'm a dedicated Souths supporter and I'd be prepared to help'. I said, 'I know you're getting great advice, just check that you do everything right, your correspondence is spot on, your figures are spot on, don't let anything go out without checking it'. And he looked at me and said…

GEORGE PIGGINS: That's good advice.

NOLENE PIGGINS: Lunch was over and he came up and he sat next to me and I knew that he was upset because he's all—you know—you know, his tie was loose and I could—I could—you know when George is upset, and he came and he whispered to me.

GEORGE: Our one little solicitor is running dead on us. We need to call together a group of other Souths lawyers… you know… all the others who have offered to help.

NICHOLAS: They had a big meeting of lawyers, about twenty lawyers came to that meeting. All the ones who'd expressed interest in volunteering. We all said a few words, I was the last to speak which was probably good, and everyone else was talking law and legalities and injunctions and I just talked about what Souths meant to me. One of those stupid, passionate speeches where passion was speaking before the brain. I said, 'We can do it, we can get an injunction. It doesn't matter, we've got the will and that's all that matters. We've got to put on the fight, it's not so much winning as putting on the fight.'

NOLENE: So that night—after that meeting, these brilliant young guys were arguing that we had a very strong case, that it was a breach of Trade Practices, right. So when—so when—George didn't get home 'til about midnight that night, and when he come home, two of the friendly barristers followed George home and said, 'Take on that young bloke, he's right'.

NICHOLAS: Then there's the Board meeting on the twentieth of October, that's when the incumbent lawyers were still retained and giving advice. They were saying that the case would cost ten million dollars and directors would lose their homes if the case was lost. Better to give up, retire the jersey into a case, there was no way they could win. Heads were down, Andrew Denton was crying, people had their heads in their hands. And Andrew was saying, 'That's basically it then, let's wrap it up now'. And this is a bit self-laudatory, and I don't want it to sound like that... so maybe someone else should say this, but basically... I got up and made this stupid, impassioned speech again, saying this was the first Souths Board meeting I'd attended, I couldn't believe what I was hearing, no one's analysed the facts, no one's analysed the Law. I turned to the lawyers and I said, 'I haven't seen one letter of advice from you, I don't know where you're coming to those conclusions from. It's very rare for a case to reach ten million dollars.' I just ranted for about five minutes and I felt the heads lifting, well, the important heads lifting, the others were looking away, the ones who were a little bit embarrassed by what they'd said.

NOLENE: George was supposed to meet me and some friends after in the Chinese restaurant. By the time he got there the lights were all out and we were waiting outside for him and we said, 'What's happened?', and he said, 'It's over. They're going to go and talk with Cronulla and I'm resigning.' And then the Board members came out and talked to George and said, 'Listen, George, we didn't vote in there. We've got a quorum here and we want to discuss it further,' and finally they said, 'Let's sleep on it tonight and we'll pursue it further'.

George went to bed and then he woke up and he was just raring to go again. He said, 'I want to call a meeting and get Nicholas appointed tonight'.

NICHOLAS: There were some significant Souths personalities who said, 'George is blindly following this cowboy solicitor who's telling him that there's a chance of success'. I wasn't stupid enough to just make promises without checking them. After those first few meetings with Souths, I had my own private meetings with a couple of very close lawyers… silks, to see if the grounds for a case existed. And they were saying, 'You might have something here'. So I wasn't acting completely rashly.

There were phone calls that I got from some very important people who recommended that I not take on the case when they heard that I was. They thought it was unwinnable and even if it was winnable, at the end of the day our opponents would get their way, so it didn't matter if I won. And it was best for my career not to do it. Why do you want to do this for? You're going to paint yourself as some fly-by-night lawyer who takes on the impossible case. It's not good for your career. Corporates won't like it. You know, that sort of thing. None of the phone calls were threatening and some of them rang, I think, out of real concern. But what annoyed me incredibly was that people were backing down because it was Murdoch, saying you just can't win. Forget about the morality or the lawfulness or anything… just give up… it's easier. And that really annoyed me. I thought, 'This is my chance to really do something'.

The essence of our court case was this. Section 45 of the Trade Practices Act says that if you and I are in competition, and you're servicing a market, and I'm servicing a market… we might be servicing parts of the same market, and then we merge. We can't then say that we will exclude certain parts of the market. We're only going to supply that part of the market. So that part that's left is left without supply.

The teams are providing the service to us. We give them a competition and they give us Rugby League services back. So that's what the case is about. Section 45 says you can't do that because you're boycotting effectively a portion of the market that is left stranded. And that's exactly what we said the reduction to fourteen teams did.

PETER MACOURT: We didn't set out to have a court case.

PLAYER: Peter Macourt. Chief Operating Officer. News Limited.

PETER: This is the problem. We'd gone down the path where St George and Illawarra had merged, Balmain and Wests had merged, Norths and Manly had merged... Um... So we'd had a whole raft of decisions made by a lot of different people in good faith based on the criteria, based on the information in front of them, based on the public and private statements of all the people involved. We couldn't get to three months before the application of the criteria and say, 'Oh, gee guys, sorry, changed our minds. What a mistake. Sorry you all had to merge. Sorry you're going to have to stay merged, but we're going to go this way now.' It just wasn't... there wasn't a way of turning back.

I was on Partnership Board and there wasn't a way of solving the problem. If we hadn't have contested Souths' claim then we were open to the claims of all the other clubs. So we were really backed into a corner. Souths just weren't in the radar until so many events had passed that... how do you... how do you unscramble the egg? It's sitting there in front of you and now what do you do about it?

PLAYER: George Piggins.

GEORGE PIGGINS: Even though we weren't strapped with cash, but we were—at that stage we were viable. You know, we were pressed for cash all the time and people kind of label us as being bad business people because they think—but, like, we never had the luxury of anybody putting in a lot of money into us.

NICHOLAS PAPPAS: We asked for an injunction pending the hearing. December 1999. That's what an injunction does, it preserves the status quo. So that we wouldn't suffer damage in the event that we won our court challenge at the end of the day. In other words, so that we could stay in the competition until we went to court. Justice Hely ruled that the balance of convenience was with the NRL and the other clubs. In other words, we had to sit out 2000.

RUPERT MURDOCH: Taken together, the activities of the past year left News Corporation better positioned than any other news and entertainment group in the world to exploit today's opportunities and to seize tomorrow's possibilities.

PLAYER: From the 1999 News Corporation Annual Report.

RUPERT: We chose as the theme for this year's annual report 'Around the World, Around the Clock'. Never has this been more true of our company than today. Virtually every minute of the day, in every time zone on the planet, people are watching, reading and interacting with our products.

We're reaching people from the moment they wake up until they fall asleep. We give them their morning weather and traffic reports through our television outlets around the world. We enlighten and entertain them with such newspapers as the *New York Post* and *The Times* as they have breakfast, or take the train to work. We update their stock prices and give them the world's biggest news stories every day through such news channels as FOX or Sky News. When they shop for groceries after work, they use our SmartSource coupons to cut their family's food bill. And when they get home in the evening, we're there to entertain them with compelling first-run entertainment on FOX entertainment on *FOX* or the day's biggest game on our broadcast, satellite and cable networks. Or the best movies from Twentieth Century Fox Film if they want to see a first-run movie. Before going to bed, we give them the latest news, and then they can crawl into bed with one of our best-selling novels from *HarperCollins*.

Our global reach and quality content have attracted people in record numbers over the past year. Indeed, fiscal 1999 was a year of 'firsts' for News Corporation.*

◆ ◆ ◆

---

* For a full list of News Corporation assets at the time of the challenge visit www.newscorp.com/report99/tvylw.html

TWO: THE SWARMING STREETS

NORM LIPSON: The first rally was just before we were kicked out and it
was to let them know, pardon my language, 'Don't fuck with us'.
PLAYER: Norm Lipson.
NORM: I don't offend you saying that, do I? Don't fuck with us. We'd
promoted it well. We'd got in the papers saying let's march for truth
and justice and all this sort of stuff. We had volunteers with flyers at
Wynyard railway station. All the major railway stations, handing
out flyers. Our rabbit in the rabbit suit, handing out flyers.

On the morning of the rally I was worried. Anything under fifteen
to twenty thousand in my opinion was a failure. Was a dead-set
failure. If we didn't get that, News Limited would have just scoffed
at us and said, 'Look, they've only got twenty people at their rally,
bugger 'em'. It really scared me. I didn't sleep the night before.

I got here about nine. And there was maybe about a hundred
people here. We're trying to pacify each other, a couple of us, saying,
you know, 'It's still early, still two hours to go, Sydney people turn
up late'. You know, making all the bloody excuses in the world.
And I just kept panicking and panicking, having anxiety attacks.
And I'll tell you something. Have you ever seen a time-lapse camera
and how that works? All of a sudden there were groups of people
coming from across the park, groups of people were coming from
the station. Bit by bit, there's a hundred people, and there's three
hundred people, and then there's five hundred people. But it still
wasn't enough. We were still panicking. Then we started getting
calls. Look, we're on a bus from Newcastle, there's seven buses
coming from Newcastle, wait for us. Trains were held up because
people just started swarming. Chalmers Street wasn't big enough to
hold everyone. There were police everywhere. CFMEU, the union
were fantastic, I've got to give them a huge rap. And then we started
marching, but it was only when we started marching and the
concertina'd crowd extended... we marched to the Town Hall up
George Street. When we got to the Town Hall I looked back and the
street was chocka block and still snaking around from Eddy Avenue.
Do you know how far that is?

PLAYER: Marcia and Barbara.

BARBARA SELBY: I went in a car that was a Parramatta car and it had the Parramatta flags on it and it had a Souths flag on it, they had a music player strapped on the roof of it and they had the South Sydney song blaring all the way over and over again into town.

MARCIA SEEBACHER: Unbelievable. You were supposed to go on a motor bike, weren't you?

BARBARA: [*laughing*] Yeah, I was supposed to go on a motor bike.

MARCIA: We had all the—like, the Harleys, they all came and donated their time to, like, people who couldn't walk.

BARBARA: Yeah, and my grand-daughter who had leukaemia, she was on one of the motor bikes, and I'm in the car and with these great big German Shepherds… [*laughing*] German Shepherds in the back of it, oh—it was just talk about—people were running along with video cameras, videoing everything, you know, and… um, people are yelling from the hotels, 'Good on youse', 'Keep it up', you know—

MARCIA: When you looked back down, back down the street, all you could see was red and green, I mean, I shouldn't say that because, no, there were flags for other clubs—

BARBARA: There were, yeah, there was Easts and Manly, Balmain—

MARCIA: Parramatta.

HELEN GRASSWILL: During the making of my television program I'd learnt that part of the strategy for trying to save the club was to organise a rally at the Town Hall.

PLAYER: Helen Grasswill.

HELEN: And I'd seen the way in which this amazing South Sydney machine worked… I mean, you don't get a rally at the Town Hall in a couple of weeks without pulling some strings. So I thought, I'll just make sure we've got some footage of this rally. Well, it turned out to the be the biggest sporting protest rally of all time. The second one superseded that. So we'd got that footage, but I hadn't necessarily decided to keep going… And I'm at this rally and watching it, and two things happened. First, a very highly-respected journalist who I'd met and who had helped me with our first story, Ian Heads, told me that day that he was resigning from the *Sunday Telegraph* because he had written a story about this rally and they'd refused to report it. And Ian said that it wasn't that they refused to run his story, it was that they refused to run any story. And it really seemed that they weren't running it because it was not in line with what the company was trying to do with Rugby League. The second thing that happened was that a number of enthusiastic Souths supporters, including a couple of Board members on that day, came up to me smiling and saying, 'Oh, now they can't kick us out, they just can't do it, this will be the front page tomorrow'. And I felt sick. And Andrew Denton, the same thing had been said to him, and he came across to me. I remember we were sitting on a stone wall and he said to me, 'What do you think?', and I said, 'I think they'll gag it', and he said, 'Yeah, so do I', and he was close to tears. I didn't have that kind of passion and I hoped I was wrong. But I was upset that the industry that I worked in, which is supposed to be fair, I didn't think it was gonna be fair.

The following day the Rugby League newspaper, the *Daily Telegraph*, owned by News Limited, ran the story on page forty-four. There was no way I was putting that story down after that.

IAN HEADS: I resigned because the *Telegraph* didn't run any story leading up to what was an entirely newsworthy event.

PLAYER: Ian Heads. Journalist and author.

IAN: It was a job and I just thought, 'I don't want to do it anymore'. So I resigned. There was a bit of drama afterwards. I did a couple of interviews. I don't even know how the word got around. I think it must be because there were a lot of sympathisers within News Limited. I took a couple of fairly angry phone calls from Phil Rothwell and John Hartigan. Honestly, what I did, I had no intention of making a fuss. Certainly there was no fear. I guess I knew I was ruffling pretty big feathers. But I felt that it had been disrespectful to Souths. They were fighting to save themselves and they'd just been ignored.

JOHN HARTIGAN: It didn't surprise me when I saw the amount of people, that was supposed to be eighty thousand, walking down George Street outside the Town Hall one Sunday afternoon.

PLAYER: John Hartigan.

JOHN: The editor of the *Telegraph* at the time says that he made a bad judgement call and that's his decision. But if the withdrawal of support, as you call it, had an effect, I wouldn't say it was tangible. Much was made of the effect that people were cancelling their Foxtel subscriptions, and cancelling their newspaper purchases and, to a degree, not going to Fox Studios. I think there's no evidence at all about Foxtel that there was any drop in subscriber base. In newspapers fluctuations of a thousand or fifteen hundred aren't unusual for all sorts of circumstances, and there was no evidence of Fox Studios suffering patronage decline.

MIKE GIBSON: Where were all these fans when their beloved Bunnies needed them most?

PLAYER: Mike Gibson.

MIKE: Sure, they're out there today. Out in their thousands, lamenting their team's exclusion from the NRL. But where were they in those last few years, when everyone in the game knew that the Rabbitohs were hanging on by the skin of their teeth? Where were they when their team was going down the gurgler, when their team was being bowled over most weekends, when Souths became the easybeats of Rugby League? They weren't there. They didn't go out to the game to show the support that would have kept their team in the competition.

THREE: HANGING ON BY A THREAD

EILEEN MCLAUGHLIN: I came to Souths as a volunteer after I took my employers to court.

PLAYER: Eileen McLaughlin. Commonly known as Nan.

EILEEN: My employer came out and he said to me, 'Eileen, you got to look at it this way, we've got to give the young ones a go'. In the end they said they'd terminate me. I took them to court for unfair dismissal. They offered me three thousand dollars, and the maximum you could get was twelve thousand five hundred. And that's what I got.

My mother died when I was six, and I was sixty-four when this case came up, and they tried to argue that my stress was about my mother's death. My son had died ten years before, he'd been dead ten years. They said that was part of it, and the fact that my other son had the same heart complaint that killed Mark. That was what my stress was about, it had nothing to do with the way I was being treated by the company! When my son died, I had a week or two weeks off and they docked me, took all my bonus off me. When the financial controller came over from head office, I had a go at him about it. 'All the years I've been here, and you have the hide to dock me when my son died.' And he said, 'Well, it's like this, if that girl over there's cat died and she wanted time off there's no difference'. I said, 'You're not comparing my son to a cat', and he said, 'No difference'. Ruthless crooks.

So that's how I come to Souths. I said to them one day, 'If you ever need any voluntary help, I've got nothing to do, it'd help me a lot'. So I used to come in and do a lot of the photocopying messages, and do all the mail-outs for them, and that was three years before we even went out. And that made a big difference to me. Coming to somewhere, even though you weren't being paid, you knew they appreciated everything you did.

Some people used to say to me, 'You'd be better off if you got paid'. I'd say, 'No, unless you've done the voluntary, you don't understand what a great feeling it is. You're doing something, but you're not expecting something back for it. It's a great fulfilment to say, "I'm not doing it for money". Everything's money money money these days. I'm doing it for the love of it and it helped me over a very big crisis.'

I love Souths. I was born and bred in the area. I met some of the greats in my younger days, Clive Churchill. Even though I moved out to the country when my ex was in the police force—Kempsey, Gundagai, Yass—and I couldn't get to the games. Eventually I came back to Sydney and I was pretty depressed in a lot of ways and my daughter says, 'Why don't you go and watch football? You love Souths, Mum.' And so my son and I started to go. My son had only just come back because my husband had taken him and my other son out of the country for thirteen years. We didn't know where they were. So when Mark and Peter came back, he was Souths too, and we've trotted off. Mark, my younger son, died of the heart condition, not my son who comes to the footy with me.

I don't think I'd still be here today without Souths. And I mean that. After I lost my job I had no self esteem, none whatsoever.

MARK COURTNEY: The day after Souths got disqualified, I got up and put on my Souths jumper as a statement of defiance, you know.

PLAYER: Mark Courtney.

MARK: That also—it also started a long period where I almost never left the house without a t-shirt or a jersey or something that identified me as a Souths supporter because I thought it was important and— I went and did the shopping that morning, you know, just walking around Franklins, and people sort of stopping you and talking to you about it, because it was a big story, and I had the Souths jumper on, and then that afternoon I drove Anya, who is my oldest daughter, to a party and… um, still had my Souths jumper on, dropped her off and one of the mums there, we talked about Souths and she said, 'They're mad'. She said, 'I saw all these people on the TV crying and they—they must be—they must be lunatics or they must —they must be—I don't know, they must just not have an idea about what's real and true in life, you know'.

And I just thought about it as I was driving home and I thought… [*pause*] that's, that's true in some ways. I just—I didn't understand it either, I really did not understand why I felt so bad and, and you know, but… [*pause*] that morning when I got up—I got up that morning… [*pause*] and I hadn't—like I'd had a few tears at the club, but I hadn't cried… [*pause*] and then my—my daughter came in and, you know, I'd taken her to the footy a couple of times and she came into my—into my bedroom just as I was sitting on the—I haven't remembered this for a long time actually—she walked into the bedroom and I was sitting on the bed and… um… [*pause*] and she said, 'Are you okay, Dad?' And I just started crying and I hugged her and I just started crying. I mean, I think it was, it's a family thing, and it's something about 'I can't give you this now, you know. Something that I've—that's mine that I should be allowed to give you and I—and I can't, you know, I'm being stopped, I've lost that, that family connection.' It's about… [*pause*] history and in the future. It's about a stream—it's a—it's a thread that goes through your life and your family's life and… ah… [*pause*] and the feeling of community and togetherness, you know. It's nice to be a part of something—it's about having anchors, is another—was another of my discoveries, you need an anchor. In fact you need about three, I reckon.

An anchor is a thing that is always going to be there, you know. If you're—you know, a practising Catholic, then it's the Catholic Church, you know, and if someone came up with a plan to merge the Catholics and the Buddhists, it wouldn't go down well, you know, because it's always been there and they know that it's always going to be there, and there's not many of those things. Australia's one, you know, but what that means, I'm not sure anymore... [*with a laugh*] but, you know, that's one. It's always going to be there, you know that it's always going to be there—I have had terrible times in life where—everyone has, you know, but I've always found... [*pause*] pretty much always that you can just escape it for a couple of hours on a Sunday, whatever was going on, you know, but you'd have to return to it, of course, but it was kind of good to be able to go there and just forget about everything else. And it's those things, it's about having anchors, and this thread that changes as—as it goes through your life.

FOUR: PEOPLE POWER

PLAYER: Marcia and Barbara.

MARCIA SEEBACHER: We were getting piles of orders, for Souths merchandise, so I'd fill them here; I'd grab a big box, and that one's a jersey, size whatever, I'd put it in the box, paperwork in it, and just load it up, load it up, load it up, just until—because, I mean, at that stage we didn't have the computer downstairs, it was all handwritten receipts— [*She laughs.*] So that's what we did, I'd sit there doing it on the machine, Mum would handwrite out the receipts, we'd make sure we doubled checked that we had everything right in the bags, off it would go, it—was all in post bags, and then the kids would sit there and they would be, like, Stephanie would write the return address on it, South Sydney, blah, blah, blah, and then—

BARBARA SELBY: By hand—

MARCIA: Yeah.

Julie Hamilton (left) as Barbara Selby and Jody Kennedy as Marcia Seebacher in the 2004 Company B production. (Photo: Heidrun Löhr)

BARBARA: Yeah, all by hand.

MARCIA: And—and—

BARBARA: After a while we got stickers.

MARCIA: We—I'd take it to the post office, drop it off at Kingsgrove—

BARBARA: Oh, can you get me some Souths stickers, bring them in, love, we don't mind doing anything for Souths, and, like, you just had so many people, just, you know, it didn't matter.

MARCIA: It was incredible.

BARBARA: The café that we went to at the court case, he joined the club and everything, joined as a football club member and as a leagues club member, because we were going in there every day and he believed, you know, like he wanted Souths in and everything, so he joined up the club and everything as well, you know, I mean—

MARCIA: I think, like, you know, again, like, we had so many people, we'd have people ringing up and they'd go, 'Oh, I'm at Menai', 'I'm at Revesby', 'I'm at—' and we'd go, 'Oh, don't worry, we'll deliver so it doesn't cost you delivery'. So we delivered so many things to so many people, like—

BARBARA: It was ridiculous, it was ridiculous when you think about it—I think—

MARCIA: I have driven with stickers in my car and seen the Souths supporters… and I've handed them out.

BARBARA: Oh, what about the day of handing it out to the truck driver?

She laughs.

MARCIA: Yeah, we've handed stickers out as we're going—

BARBARA: As we've stopped at the traffic lights—

MARCIA: Because you've got Souths stickers on your car, and I go, 'I've got some here'—

BARBARA: It was Bambi and Simone, I think, who got the stickers going, and because they—it was a good money-spinner, like two dollars or one dollar a sticker, or whatever, and, I mean, they just went like hotcakes, and then were was times that they'd say, 'Okay, we're just going to give these stickers out', so everyone would take piles of them and then no one else could get them because they were free, like—

MARCIA: And what about the day they—that—that… um, thousands and thousands of them, they'd spent—they'd spelt the Rabbitohs wrong, they put 'Rabbit toes'—

BARBARA: 'Rabbit toes', so we had to cut—

MARCIA: We had to cut them—

BARBARA: We'd cut the emblem off so that—

MARCIA: The emblem because—

BARBARA: And that was thousands—

MARCIA: I used to take them home and cut them up and, oh—

BARBARA: We couldn't do it, like—

MARCIA: It was, like, 'Throw them out', it was, like, throwing them out, so we're going, 'But we could sell these'—

BARBARA: 'We'll sell these for a dollar.'

MARCIA: So we… sell… for a dollar.

BARBARA: And… um, you know, people loved it, they just loved the little stickers.

MARCIA: Oh, people couldn't get enough stickers.

BARBARA: And they'd say to me, 'Oh, but haven't you got any of those little ones that I've seen?' 'Oh, hang on and I'll get you some', and I'd grab some from underneath and cut them up for them.

MARCIA: People come down from Queensland, Townsville, saying, 'I'm down from Townsville, I need a hundred stickers because people up there just want to spread the word', and—

BARBARA: You couldn't get enough.

MARCIA: [laughing] And you'll see, still see 'em now, she'll go, 'Oh, there's my sticker'.

BARBARA: [laughing] Yeah—

MARCIA: It's quite funny.

BARBARA: Because I said to the—because, you know, I've said to Simone, 'No, we'll cut them. Choom, like that. We've got little rabbits.'

MARCIA: And they sold like hot—we couldn't have—get enough of them.

BARBARA: Yeah.

MARCIA: People that had just heard from, like, you say England and whatever, and they'd—

BARBARA: Texas—

MARCIA: —just seen it on the Net and the amount of things we sent to Texas, like, why did we send—Texas, like, I mean—

BARBARA: We had—and a princess, or a prince or something—

MARCIA: A prince, a prince in the Fijian islands.

BARBARA: A member, yeah, a member of the football club.

MARCIA: He was a Fijian island, or some island in Fiji, and he was a prince.

BARBARA: He became a member of the football club.

MARCIA: Yeah, he was, I don't know if he still is, but—

BARBARA: Maybe—

MARCIA: I mean we also had things—

BARBARA: It was unbelievable.

MARCIA: —disappearing, so you knew there were people that were even Souths supporters that were really against you because, like, we'd have merchandise over the sales, and people would steal things and—

BARBARA: Oh, there's always one.

MARCIA: Always one.

BARBARA: Oh, that's because they can get it for nothing.

MARCIA: We won't forget him either.

BARBARA: No.

MARCIA: We won't forget his name, we know who he is.

BARBARA: Mobile phone and—

MARCIA: Stole Brandon's mobile phone, yes.

BARBARA: It's just when you talk about it and you go back and you think, 'Gosh, how many nights I did sit up till eleven o'clock—?'

MARCIA: Yeah, it's like when you're in the middle of it, you're not realising, but now that you sit back, you just—

BARBARA: Yeah, well that's it—

MARCIA: Sit back and think of all the, you know—I learnt that I could communicate with people—

BARBARA: Yes.

MARCIA: After being a mum for so long, you sort of, you feel worthless, like you're no good at anything.

BARBARA: Yes.

MARCIA: So, yeah, you sort of—

BARBARA: Well, it's a sort of—

MARCIA: Yeah, definitely.

BARBARA: Yeah, it's given you a lot of confidence and it—you know, sort of, well, it gave me something too—well, it made me realise that I could still do things—

MARCIA: Yes, that's it.

BARBARA: And yeah, yeah. And I think, you know, my customer service skills were very handy throughout the fight because it, you know, you knew how to communicate with people and, you know, if you had to ring people and say, 'Oh, look, I'm sorry but we can't fill this order', well, you knew how to talk to them and, yeah.

MARCIA: Well, you sort of had—we were like the face of Souths in some way.

BARBARA: Oh, we were, yes.

MARCIA: A few people that would ring up and complain about—'Oh, I spoke to someone and they don't want to help me' raah, but they'd say, 'Oh, Barbara, helped me', so I go, 'Oh, that's my mum'.

She laughs.

BARBARA: Yeah, so you did get a few people that were—they really appreciated what you did for them.

MARCIA: Yes, yes.

BARBARA: And, I mean, we did, we bent over backwards—

MARCIA: We did, we did bend over backwards for people because we knew that they believed in what we believed in and… um—

BARBARA: Like I said, like, 'We're in Queensland, we can't do it, we'd be helping you if we could', and the only way they could help was buy merchandise and they did it.

MARCIA: No. Actually I've still got, actually I've still got this man's name, this is from last year, he wants a phone cover, he's in Queensland and he can't find a phone cover, and I just haven't found one.

BARBARA: You've still got it in your handbag?

MARCIA: I've still got it because I keep thinking—and I've been to Queensland and I thought, 'Oh, gosh, I wish I could find one and take it up to him', but anyway, I'll keep it because one day I will ring him out of the blue when I find them.

TELEGRAPH: Souths have launched an investigation after a mystery hacker erased their website database, costing the embattled club thousands of dollars in fundraising money.

PLAYER: As reported in the *Daily Telegraph*.

TELEGRAPH: The club's merchandising site has been offline for a week and the contact details of people wanting to order stock or tickets to next month's fundraising concert have been lost.

PLAYER: George Piggins.

GEORGE: We were getting revenue of seven hundred dollars a day before this. This is a real setback for us. It's been deliberately done and I can't see how any Souths supporter could have done this.

BRYAN RAYNER: Oh, they were certainly very upset, their morale was down as a whole district.

PLAYER: Father Bryan Rayner.

RAYNER: Right at the peak of Souths fightback I preached at all the masses on one particular Sunday about Souths, and surprisingly at some of the masses there was a great deal of applause after the sermon. You don't get that too often, so that was rather a thrill. The military bishop, he's a very keen Souths supporter... um, in fact he's so keen that his mitre is red and green as well, and he grew up in Maroubra parish and... ah—he got involved in some of their Save Souths campaigns, and I think in one of the speeches he gave at a rally, he made the comment that... um, 'Rugby League without South Sydney is like the Catholic Church without the Pope'. So... um, it was good—good to see that support from the religious side.

And also I mentioned at another mass later... um, or at other masses, that about nine of the Catholic bishops of Australia had signed a petition... um, which basically was supporting South Sydney. The general thing was that they thought it wrong that in the interests of multi-nationalism or of greed, that the interests of particular sporting clubs were being neglected, and after they heard that, when I announced that the bishops supported it, the congregation broke into applause again. So... um, it's good sometimes that... ah, the views of the Church are seen to—seen to be very popular. South Sydney and the Catholic Church have been caught up in a lot of things over many years and I think... ah, they think the same—certainly on justice in sport.

END OF ACT TWO

ACT THREE

ONE: FORTY DAYS AND FORTY NIGHTS

PHIL PIKE: Our barrister was Tom Hughes.

PLAYER: Phil Pike.

PHIL: Tom walks in, right, and he got a shock when he seen all these supporters there and the gallery full and they're in their red and green and passin' around bags of lollies and outside is full. And his glasses are sittin' down here and he walked around and he looked around and he opened the case up and he goes, 'Your Honour. This is a class of people, Your Honour. Some people like opera.' Which is the judge. He liked opera. See, so he turned round. 'Some people like cricket. These people like football.'

An' he goes… 'These people are tribal, Your Honour. They are a class of people, Your Honour.' An'… an' we all sat there and, and we're all just starin' at this bloke thinkin', 'Oh yeah, well, yeah yeah, we're a class of people, that's true'. An' we were. We all sat there watchin' this court case, watchin' these TV monitors that no one ever knew anything about. Couldn't understand it. When all the money people got on the stand, someone'd say, 'What's this bloke got to do with us bein' in the comp?' 'Oh, he's telling him why the finances are this, this and that.' 'Oh, get rid of 'im, piss 'im off, we don't want 'im. 'Oo's the next witness this arvo?' 'Won't be no more today. Be tomora.' 'Oh, okay, I'm goin 'ome early, go 'ome and do me 'usband's tea and me housework. I'll see yas tomorrow.' And off they'd go and they'd come back. Next day, ''Oo's on today?' There was a lady, used to come every day from Windsor to sit and watch the court case. She used to get up at five-thirty in the morning, put all her washing on, do all the housework, get the kids to school and come into the court.

It was so funny, one day, I'll never forget this day. I was sitting down in the Botanical Gardens having lunch with a friend of mine.

And hold me blown, who's walkin' around? Justice Paul Finn. And he turned around and he went, 'Hello, how are you?', and I said, 'How are you?', and he said, 'I'll see you in court', and I said, 'I'll be there'. [*He laughs.*] He seen me every day sittin' in the court with Nicholas.

NICHOLAS PAPPAS: Every day people rang wanting to talk to me. Every lawyer who was a Souths supporter wanted to join in.

PLAYER: Nicholas Pappas.

NICHOLAS: There were two limbs to the case... there was the Trade Practices side and there was the contract side. That they'd dealt with us unfairly. We wanted... we knew all along that it was a difficult case... but we knew that we'd uncover a lot of material that would reach the public domain, because once it's said in open court it's in the public domain despite any confidentiality orders... would reach the public domain about how they'd favoured other clubs, how much money they'd given other clubs while complaining that Souths had no money... that there was an agenda to keep some clubs up and discard others. That was very much about the moral victory... and George was determined to get that stuff out because he wanted to give people the encouragement to keep... keep believing in the fight.

We were here late at night trying to fix the photocopier. The fax machine nearly blew up with the amount of paper that they were throwing at us. News, NRL, ARL and the clubs, we said, were all in one interest and therefore should have retained one firm of lawyers, but what they did was retain separate firms... Allens, the biggest firm in Australia, NRL retained Minter Ellison, effectively the second-biggest firm in Australia, the clubs retained Henry, Davis, York, another very large firm, and the ARL retained its own solicitors. So the prospects for us of costs orders was huge. And so that was a frightening prospect.

Did we lose sleep? We worked through the night here many times. I had a barrister camped in my Board room full-time, a junior barrister on our team working here full-time because I didn't have the resources and I had to keep this practice running. I had a para-legal working full-time and I had one secretary working full-time. And one day we got twenty-six incoming faxes from the appellants...

and all long, detailed faxes that you had to respond to immediately to protect your client's interest… and I remember we lined them up on the Board table and I said, 'How are we going to answer these today?' And we did. We worked through the night and within a day or so we'd answered them… and, you know, the solicitors on the other side actually said, 'We actually thought you'd drown in the sea of paper. We actually thought you would. That you'd collapse. Eventually.' Yeah. I'm not saying the tactics they used weren't legitimate… they used every legitimate tactic under the sun… every stalling tactic, every tactic that would put us to further costs, every tactic that would intimidate us.

PLAYER: George Piggins.

GEORGE PIGGINS: Six weeks into this hearing, which lasted forty days and forty nights, we was asked to pass what became known as a 'fertility test'. We… look, basically we'd shown them a plan for the Rabbitohs' entire operation for the next five years. We said we could raise twenty million dollars in sponsorship. 'Prove that you can raise half that amount', says Justice Finn.

ANDREW DENTON: We basically had two weeks to raise, I think it was eight million dollars.

PLAYER: Andrew Denton.

ANDREW: Minimum eight, and… ah, we'd scraped together about five and… um, people wanted to do stuff, but the attitude was, 'It's too big. You can't fight City Hall.' Ah, but this friend of mine said, 'You know, you should talk to Kerry Stokes because he feels quite passionate about this'.

I'd written to Kerry earlier in the year saying… ah… [pause] 'I—I understand that you're interested in Souths'… I said, 'I may want to talk to you at some point', not realising quite what that would mean, and—and he said, 'That's fine'.

So when the moment came, I rang up and, you know—it's one of those things where it's, like, you can only ask, you can only ask— and it was a party line and Mike Whitney was on the other line, and I said, 'Kerry, I—you know what's happening with Souths', I explained where we were at the court case, and I said, 'Basically, Kerry, we need to have this money in two weeks, I'm ringing up to ask if you will sponsor us for a million dollars a year for three years'.

And he just said, 'Yes', and… ah, it was a very brief phone call, and I said, 'Well, we'll—Nick will be in touch, we obviously need to get documents signed', and I think two nights later we went to meet him. But it was—he was just—he said, he said to me, he said, 'Look, I really—' what was it he said? 'I really believe that… ah, that the people that own the club should have a right to keep them', and you know, I've—as I said, I think Kerry Stokes is a most unusual man in this position. I'm sure he's a ruthless and very good businessman, because he's not where he is for no reason… he's no fool, the highest-rating *Today Tonight* ever was the night they broadcast from Souths when they were axed. But I don't think that's why Kerry Stokes did it. I also know that the moment this was announced, he copped extreme pressure, direct from New York, about what he'd done.

So, really, he was on a hiding to nothing and… um, you know, I don't think the club… ah, it's my only real regret in all of this, I don't think the club treated him at all well. I don't think they've paid him his due. I don't think they have welcomed, honoured him as they should, and I feel really embarrassed about that, and very upset about it. Um… [*pause*] and that to me is—this is a whole other subject, but that to me is the core of what's wrong with Souths—

They don't understand—there is something special about Souths, but that doesn't mean they don't have to… ah, respond to the world properly. But that's another can of worms.

NICHOLAS PAPPAS: I remember getting the call from Stokes' publicity guy who said that he'd just got a call from Murdoch's publicity guy in New York and the words were, 'Rupert's gone ballistic that Kerry's got involved'… What's he doing in his backyard? And we thought, 'Oh God, war's really on now. This is bigger than all of us now'… But, y'know, we started to realise, 'God, this means a lot more than just Rugby League, may even be more than pay TV, now it's getting down to the egos'.

PHIL PIKE: The thing that really, really pissed me off as a supporter…

PLAYER: Phil Pike.

PHIL: … that made me really proud as a club person. I seen people comin' in putting money in that I knew they couldn't afford that money. They were battlin' people puttin' that money in an' that's a disgrace. And here's a multi-multi-million-dollar company who make… To them it was just business. But it wasn't business to us. I tell you. We didn't need to look at the calendar to know what day pension day was on. When most of the people who came in the joint to put money in. They were buying all the Souths clothes. Their wardrobe was full of Souths clothes. When Rupert says to his finance guy, 'Write me a million-dollar cheque', he probably doesn't even think about it. But when we gave our money, people put their savings in. Saved up for renovations… didn't do 'em… put it into the fightback.

TWO: DOWN THE RABBIT HOLE

TELEGRAPH: South Sydney Rugby Leagues Club is ready for its biggest party ever today… or 'one hell of a wake'.

PLAYER: *Daily Telegraph.*

TELEGRAPH: The Redfern Club will be the base for the Rabbitohs red and green army of supporters when the Federal Court rules on Souths' future in the NRL at ten-fifteen a.m..

TOM COCKING: We had calls from people in Newcastle saying they were leaving home at four a.m. to be here in time.

PLAYER: Tom Cocking, Souths Leagues Club Manager.

TOM: It was going to be the biggest crowd we had ever had in this new club. Morale was high. We hoped the courts would have a bit of compassion.

NORM LIPSON: The club put up a large screen in the auditorium to show the telecast of the court decision.

PLAYER: Norm Lipson.

NORM: And we also put on an early breakfast for supporters. The Federal Court also opened an extra courtroom for supporters where they could watch on closed circuit TV Justice Paul Finn's decision.

JUSTICE PAUL FINN: In our view Rugby League is an icon to be preserved for the people who love and support it, not a product to be carved up to the media for their own financial gratification.

Several of the players cheer and scream.

I am quoting from correspondence submitted by the South Sydney Football Club. However, it is usually only fortuitous that some legal principle can be found that could provide such preservation as is sought. This is not one of the fortuitous cases.

There is a shocked silence.

The NRL were not acting, and had not acted, in the circumstances, in ways that no reasonable person could act. They were making complex judgements in novel and difficult circumstances in which they knew they could not please everyone.

NORM: He said that the reduction of teams to fourteen meant no substantial lessening of competition. And he said that even if the criteria was applied wrongly it didn't mean the NRL's intentions in reducing the competition weren't honourable. Then he said that as far as the Law was concerned, tradition was about as relevant as preserving a fart in a glass jar. We'd lost the case. We'd lost. And we were out.

Long pause.

ALAN CATT: 'Allow me to point out a few salient facts to the whingeing Souths Sydney Rugby League supporters. If your club wasn't so arrogant you would have amalgamated and kept part of your identity as many others have. The average premiership crowd figure this year was the highest in many seasons despite missing the precious Rabbitohs. Souths crowds for most of the 1990s were pathetic before you looked like getting the boot. Souths results for the 1990s were pathetic.' Alan Catt, of Redfern. In a letter to the *Telegraph*.

P. GERAGHTY: 'Can someone honestly tell me why Souths actually deserve to be in the competition? In the last twelve seasons they have made the finals only once, claiming more wooden spoons than in a chef's kitchen. Supporters keep claiming that the Bunnies have won the most premierships, but people don't seem to realise that their premierships were won when only six to eight teams contested the premiership. When are league supporters going to acknowledge that what the NRL has done is for the good of the game?' P. Geraghty, of Maroubra.

JEFF COOK: 'I feel sad for the supporters of South Sydney. The writing was on the wall for a long time and, while I am sympathetic to Souths, they have no one to blame but themselves. For some reason they think themselves different from Balmain, Wests, Norths and St George. These clubs had the foresight to be pro-active in deciding their future. However, too much water has gone under the bridge. The George

Piggins faction of 'swim alone or not at all' will now bear the fruits of its folly. Farewell, Souths, you should have been more flexible when the opportunity arose.' Jeff Cook, West Pennant Hills.

Pause.

ANDREW DENTON: After the first court case, on the day of the announcement, I was, I was sitting next to Craig Coleman.

PLAYER: Andrew Denton.

ANDREW: And... um, you know, you just knew straight away from the way that... ah, Finn was speaking, that it was gone and... ah, but Tugger, Coleman, I remember Tugger when Finn made his announce—judgement, which was probably quick, Tugger said, 'Have we won?'. It was like... ahhhhh, 'No, no, that's not a win'. I remember what really struck in my core was his words, 'the case was not sufficiently fortuitous'... [*pause*] and... ah, I wrote an article to the *Herald* after that... [*pause*] which was... ah, which said, you know, this is, you know, forgive us for being angry but... ah, you know, in a city where... [*pause*] John Laws walks free because he's too famous to be jailed, and where, you know, in a country where Christopher Skase... ah, can't be brought back to justice, and Alan Bond pays one cent in every hundred dollars... ah, why is it that Souths' case is not sufficiently fortuitous?

EILEEN MCLAUGHLIN: I didn't have a lot of faith in the justice system. I thought, 'There's no justice in this country'.

PLAYER: Eileen McLaughlin.

EILEEN: Souths then had to get rid of most of their staff, they couldn't afford to pay staff because everything had to go into the fight.

GEORGE PIGGINS: I think that they're prepared to take sport away from the working class and they say more or less you can't afford to come to the game, you go home and watch it on TV.

PLAYER: George Piggins.

GEORGE: You want kids to play sport, you want kids to look up to sport, and you want sportsmen to be a role model and maybe, you know, like, instead of kids getting off their—their—you know, like, if there's not a side like South Sydney to aspire to, even if we have one kid drifting to drugs because of it, it's one too many, and all that kind of structure was just being eroded for the dollar.

Like, to go to the Sydney Football Stadium, it can cost you a—
your wife, yourself, your wife, two kids—ah, out of the rain, it can
cost you the best, by the time you park your car, a few pies, over a
hundred dollars. Well, the average bloke can't afford that. But, like…
ah, they—they just shut us out and took something off us which we
believe in, in the Law.

BARBARA SELBY: Even up until he said no, I thought he was going to
say yes.

PLAYER: Barbara Selby.

BARBARA: I really thought that he was, and I just sort of… [*pause*] I
was stunned and I walked out of the courtroom and I walked out the
front and it wasn't until I got to the front steps and someone said
something to me that it hit me, that we'd lost and… [*pause*] it was
just unbelievable, I—I don't know, I just broke down then and they
just, you know, because as soon as you show tears, the media
everywhere, you know. Well, it was proven that—that they didn't
come near you unless you were being emotional—

PLAYER: Marcia Seebacher.

MARCIA SEEBACHER: Because I didn't get on TV very much, I held it all
in until I was out of sight. I was lucky.

BARBARA: Because that day, who was there that—oh, Simone, took me
over and put me in the Rabbit Van and—and even when we got in
the van, they had the camera right in the van and someone said,
'Oh, get away, can't you get away, can't you see these people have
had enough?' You know.

NICHOLAS PAPPAS: The first court loss I remember driving out to the
club and thinking, 'What am I going to say to these people?'

PLAYER: Nicholas Pappas.

NICHOLAS: Y'know? I got the phone call that there's three thousand people
waiting to be spoken to. I didn't know if we had the right to appeal.
I hadn't had a chance to look at the judgement, which was this thick.
There was chaos at the court room. November 2000, 'What do I tell
these people?' I was driving there thinking this is the worst day of
my life. This is definitely the worst day of my life. And sort of the
despondency I'd seen in court, by the time I got out there, everyone
was celebrating, they were joyous again. They were there cheering

when we got on the stage. And there were some great speeches made that day. And it was easy. I just got up there and said, you know, 'We're going to appeal'. Without knowing if we could. And everyone went, 'Yeah, we're going to appeal'. And this was the aftermath of just a total loss. Finn knocked us out on every point. And it just made them more determined.

THREE: ALL OR NOTHING

GEORGE PIGGINS: We're launching an appeal against Justice Finn's decision. We won't play First Division next year. We are not going away. We'll go on as long as we can to get ourselves back in the competition. We have one more shot at it. Hopefully that will be successful. Meanwhile we have to find a way to raise more funds.

NOLENE PIGGINS: I always did, you know, an annual ball, yeah, for the Red and Green Ball.

PLAYER: Nolene Piggins.

NOLENE: So that, that, that, had been… um, my function. I mean, it's grown to probably, you know, we probably get about a thousand people at that function. Yes, so anyway… um, it went ahead and we raised, you know, something like four hundred thousand, but I found that night how—the sort of support we had, because we were at Darling Harbour, and seventeen hundred and fifty people in Darling Harbour, and we turned hundreds away. We sold out pretty quickly.

BARRY MURRAY: I put together a 'Souths Bash in the Bush' weekend in Scone.

PLAYER: Barry Murray.

BARRY: A thirty-five-dollar-a-head dinner in the Scone Golf Club. And the guest speaker, you wouldn't believe it, the guest speaker was John Sattler. Sattler! In Scone! Then we had a fundraising golf tournament, twenty dollars a head, plus lunch. With Craig Coleman, Les Davidson, Terry Fahey, Darryl Neville and Ziggy Niscott.

PLAYER: Phil Pike.

PHIL PIKE: We had a team that went to all the country areas. We went to Dubbo and we went to Wagga Wagga. I was the team manager of that tour. Got them their hotel, told 'em when training was on. We

went to Newcastle. We played in Maitland. We played there. And
the people came out to see us. And we still knew we was alive.
Me and the other volunteers. We worked two and a half years.
Every day. I worked in there every day. I had Christmas Day and
Boxing Day off. And that's it. Like, some days I get up and go in
there. I'd be in there by nine o'clock in the morning and I'd leave by
five o'clock, sometimes six o'clock. Sometimes ten o'clock at night.
Every now and then, every fortnight on a Thursday I'd go in there at
eleven o'clock. And before I went in there, I'd go to St George
Hospital, because I'm on dialysis every day now. Then it was every
two weeks. I used to go in there, get my treatment, and then, bang,
hop in my car and go into Souths.

Like, an' I remember the day we lost, and there's this bloke on
TV. Standin' there in tears. They kicked his football team out. An'
he went home and he threw out every little bit of *Telegraph* stuff
that he had in his house. He said, 'You threw my football team out,
Rupert, and I'll throw you out'. A friend of mine who lives on the
Northern Beaches. An' this bloke knocks at the front door one day
and he says, 'Oh, good afternoon, sir, how you going?'. He says,
'I'm a Foxtel blah blah blah blah', and this bloke, he goes, 'Can you
wait one minute, mate?'. And he says, 'Yeah, sure, mate'. An' he
goes out and gets this picture off the wall and he brings it to the
front door and he says, 'You come to this house. Mate. Do you
know who that is?'. And the bloke stood there and he looks at it and
he says, 'Is that your father?'. And this guy goes, 'That's John Sattler,
mate'. And this bloke looks at him and he goes... [*pause*] 'Oh no. Oh
no, you're a Souths supporter, aren't you?'. And this man says, 'Yes'.
And he gave him this barrage. And the Foxtel guy says, 'I've gotta
go'. An' the fan says, 'Don't go to that house two doors up, and don't
go there, and don't go there'. And this is on the Northern Beaches.

The day we got kicked out, if you would a drove around Kensington,
Maroubra, Revesby, you seen all these Foxtel transformers out on
the street. They rung up to get them collected and if they didn't
come they just put it out the front. You could of just come and took
it and put it in your home and you would have been sweet.

Mate. I remember a particular bloke who followed Souths, he
turned around and he, dead-set, he, dead-set, did not... would not

eat for about three or four days after we lost that court case. And he was just so emotionally wrecked. He never went to work. He never went to work and he turned around an' the poor bloke... he was shattered. He was absolutely shattered. Football was his life. He watched Souths in Newcastle. He watched them in Canberra. An' his wife turned around and he stood there in the kitchen and I remember I said to him very clearly. I said, 'Mate, look look look look, the game of Rugby League is not worth doin' your marriage over'. He's got three kids. She turned around and said, 'Look, wake up to yourself'. She says, 'This is just a football team'. He shouts, 'A football team? You stupid woman!'. And they had this massive argument in the kitchen.

I know a bloke who's got some turf. Who collected turf from Redfern Oval. And he waters it every day. He waters it every day. An' he does. He's got it in this big frame at his house. In his backyard. I said, 'What have you got that for, you dope?', and he said, 'Mate. You gotta be kiddin'.' He said, 'This is the greatest grass in the world, mate. The greatest players in the world played on this.'

NORM LIPSON: The mood of the city... it just turned.

PLAYER: Norm Lipson.

NORM: It was, like, every sandwich shop you went into, every pub, every Board room, every street corner, they were talking about Souths. And they weren't talking about Rugby League. They were talking about the banks. And the police stations. And they were talking about how many times Souths had been told we were dead in the water and then fought on. It was about identifying something you really believe in. How many times in your life are you that sure? And suddenly it wasn't just a Rugby League team who were sure, it was city who were sure. A whole city. And Souths just became the rabbit that roared.

PLAYER: The Courtney family.

ANYA: Well, when Souths were out, Dad was a lot more sad, and we had to boycott a lot of things.

PLAYER: Anya, eleven. Bronte, nine. Freya, seven. Cindy Hawkey, Mark Courtney's wife.

ANYA: We had to have this... sultana...

BRONTE: Sultana…

ANYA: Sanitarium. Fake Nutri-grains and they weren't very nice.

BRONTE: When we got back onto real Nutri-grains it was a relief.

ANYA: Most of the time I was happy to go along with it.

BRONTE: That was when we just had toast.

CINDY HAWKEY: My poor, deprived children. [*She laughs.*] Freya was in pre-school and she did get invited to a party at Fox Studios at Lollypops, and it was quite important for her to go because she'd started a new pre-school and she didn't know many of the kids, and I thought she should go because it would help her to get to know some of the kids, and Anya gave her a bad time about going.

ANYA: I don't remember that.

FREYA: I do.

CINDY: I was all for her going to Fox Studios to make new friends and that sort of thing. I knew how important it was to Mark.

MARK COURTNEY: I went and had a long talk to her and said, 'You know, look, you need to understand that if you go to the party, firstly, it won't impact Souths' chances of getting back into the competition, and secondly, I won't be disappointed, so don't be doing it because of that, but this is one of those times where you have to, you know, make some choices about—and—and these things happen all through your life, you know, and, you know, that's why boycotts and things are hard. That's why these sorts of things are hard. You know, it's easy to say you'll do it, but—and it's easy to do it for a while, but something will happen, like this, where it's hard and that's where the real test comes and, you know, it's up to you, but either way it will be okay.' And she didn't go.

CINDY: Not having McDonalds wasn't a problem.

BRONTE: Because you can just go to Burger King.

CINDY: Not having Kelloggs wasn't a problem either.

ANYA *groans.*

I don't share that passion. I don't have the same sort of passion as he does. For anything really. Mark still has trouble ringing Greg if he can't make the football, though. Like, if something comes up… like, if we have a wedding to go to… that we just have to go to… Mark just dreads ringing Greg.

GREG WILKINSON: I always thought it was more if he was just going out to dinner with friends.

PLAYER: Greg Wilkinson.

GREG: I thought… but if it was family things… I hopefully… [*He hesitates.*] I probably was that bad.

> CINDY *laughs.*

It changed my life when Souths were out. I went from watching half a dozen games of Rugby League in a weekend and talking to Mark a dozen times a week about the game and reading newspapers and magazines, to doing gardening on a Sunday afternoon with my wife. Which is just… we almost got divorced! I was miserable most of the time. In some ways it was good to spend a winter with Sue, which I hadn't ever done…

> CINDY *laughs.*

From left rear: Eliza Logan (seated) as Nolene Piggins and (standing) Georgina Naidu as Cindy Hawkey, Josef Ber as Mark Courtney and Russell Kiefel as Greg Wilkinson; from left, seated on floor: Alex Sideratos as Anya Courtney, Julie Hamilton as Freya Courtney and Jody Kennedy (foreground) as Bronte Courtney in the 2004 Company B production. (Photo: Heidrun Löhr)

I'd been with her since I was seventeen, so it's almost thirty years now, forty-six now. It was an awful time. And I was never going to live the dream of winning a Grand Final and celebrating that with Mark and, look, that's my dream. It's like other people climbing a mountain. This was my dream. Mark is family to me and to have that not be there...

CINDY: I quite enjoy the time when Mark goes to the footy and takes the kids to the footy because it means I get to have time to myself. It's time that I can have. If I go the footy it's, 'I want to go to the toilet, Mum'. But if Dad takes them, it's Dad. So I have some time to myself and I like that. When they were out I didn't have that.

CAROLINE JONES: Dear Lachlan. It might help if I explain a few things about Australians, so you can understand why people are saying they hope you rot in hell.

PLAYER: Caroline Jones. Author and television presenter.

CAROLINE: They say we're still not sure what our identity is, but try taking it away from us and you'll soon find out what it is. I'm sorry to go against what your father taught you, Lachlan, but there are some things that money can't buy, though it surprises me to say it. When you do a thing that makes Australian men cry, you know you're on the wrong track. And the way we see it, what's the point of being the richest kid in the world if people like George Piggins say you're a mongrel? It's a terrible thing to be called. All the best for your future. Caroline.

ROBERT TAYLOR: I felt utter disgust while they was out.

PLAYER: Robert Taylor. Souths Juniors referee.

ROBERT: The government's attitude is this. You be good little darkies and we'll look after you. Not letting us look after ourselves like we could if we're given the opportunity. It won't change in my lifetime. I don't believe that it'll ever change. Because the governments that they put into parliament are so racist and biased... they ought to look beyond what they're seein'. Ya... you take the notification of ANZAC. What basically is ANZAC? They will recognise a war that our people went overseas for, but they won't recognise the slaughter of the Aboriginal people within Australia itself. The many wars on Aboriginal people, the rights taken away. That's why I never

call myself an Australian. But I'll call myself a South Sydney
supporter. Because it weren't 'til 1968 that we had recognisation as
an Australian. 1968, I was fourteen years old. So before that I weren't
recognised as an Australian. But I was recognised as a Souths fan,
so I'll stick with them. One year, it was a Grand Final, I don't
remember what year it was, but it was Souths playin' St George.
And it was overcrowded... before they put all the stands and that
up, it was just a hill there. And... um, I collapsed in the crowd... So
the Souths people, they called an ambul... first aid, and they passed
me across the fence and they carried me right down the other side of
the oval where the privileged people were, that's where I was sittin'.
And I stayed there for the whole game. Just overheated because it
was packed. Upper-class stand. And I sat there all the game. And
that was before my people even had the vote. I still won't recognise
myself as an Australian. An' that's what Souths means to me. So if
they wanted to take it away. That's what it means.

Pause.

Wayne Blair as Robert Taylor in the 2004 Company B production.
(Photo: Heidrun Löhr)

JOHN HARTIGAN: Some of our people were subjected to constant death threats.

PLAYER: John Hartigan.

JOHN: So whatever you make of it, I guess you're always going to have these influences. It's easy to look upon it as just a group of footy fans against a corporate player. It really became a very, very nasty piece of work, which I guess any argument and brawl does.

NICHOLAS PAPPAS: We had appealed Justice Finn's decision on the grounds that he had erred nine times in his November judgement.

PLAYER: Nicholas Pappas.

NICHOLAS: He had found that the exclusion of Souths was an unfortunate side product of an otherwise honourable intention. [*He grimaces.*] So we had to go back to the Full Bench, three judges this time, and argue that the NRL and News did know that there would be this effect, and that the reduction to fourteen teams was their primary purpose, in itself, as a purpose.

The appeal lasted three days. And the fans were there again, though the numbers were down.

On the last day of the appeal trial, one of Souths' most devoted supporters brought in a tray of baked goods. She'd been there every day in her red and green, and she'd often brought in home-made cookies and the like. This day it was freshly-made vanilla slices. So she came into the court and she offered them around to everyone, and they looked fantastic, so we were all sitting there eating them. And then she looked over to the opposing bar table and, without thinking, went over to opposing Counsel and offered them a slice. They looked at the vanilla slices and they really wanted to take one, but they didn't know if it was quite right. But the woman looked at them and said, 'Go on, have one'. And so they did.

And we all sat in court, fifteen barristers at one end of the table and our two at the other end, all eating home-made vanilla slices. It was this wonderful moment, and they started to smile and just relaxed for a second, all sitting round in a circle, after trying to murder each other for two years, you know. It was like one of those moments from the First World War, you know, Christmas time when they would shake the Germans' hands and it all seems so ridiculous and pointless. 'Surely there's a compromise here somewhere', you feel like saying... and you wish just for a moment that it was that easy.

FOUR: THE TRUE BELIEVERS

PLAYER: Barbara and Marcia.

BARBARA SELBY: When we had the—the three judges, the appeal trial, I thought, 'Well, three heads are better than one, and there's got to be someone that Murdoch can't get at', and that was how we felt, like, I mean, I, in particular, felt that... um, somehow or other he'd got to—

MARCIA SEEBACHER: Everyone.

BARBARA: Justice Finn and, you know—

MARCIA: But the poor man probably had nothing to do with it.

BARBARA: Probably didn't, but—

MARCIA: We blame him anyway.

BARBARA: —that's how we feeled, how we felt, you know—I just felt that we had a really big chance with the appeal—I felt more confident really and... um—then when we got in there, the day that the decision was handed down, I thought when he started to speak, I thought, 'Oh—I don't know'... [pause] because he was, like—

MARCIA: We'd actually heard that only one judge had to read it and then discuss with the others, so I just thought, 'Well, what's the point of having three judges?', like—

BARBARA: Yeah—

MARCIA: —if it's just one judge, but anyway, I don't know whether that was—

BARBARA: —and he said he would not grant the appeal or something, but... [pause] one judge would grant—would say we'd won, and... [pause] and the third one said, 'And I will grant it', yeah. He said, 'In which case Souths has succeeded on its appeal'. So that's a yes.

> The others erupt on stage. Some say 'yes' loudly, others find it quietly.

I—we're at the court and I'm trying to ring Marcie, and trying to ring my son and all the family, I had all the—all these calls I had to make, and you couldn't get a call out on your mobile, oh, it was dreadful.

MARK COURTNEY: We were all in the bloody auditorium.

PLAYER: Mark Courtney.

MARK: At the club, there would have been a few hundred, there weren't thousands, there might have been four hundred, I don't know, three hundred or something, I don't know, and I was sitting there feeling sick... and the, the coverage was starting. The Channel Seven, whatever they had on the big screen, the—you know, the logo or whatever—and they were about to start the coverage. Simone's phone rang and she was talking on it and we—nobody was watching the screen, everybody was watching her—and she was standing there going, 'Yeah, yep, yep', and she just threw the phone in the air and said, 'We won'... had this—it was—it was quite—I still get excited when thinking about it, I still feel the elation of the moment. I thought, 'My God, my God'... and the part that I played was bigger than I ever thought... um, I could do, and—and I've got it there for my—for my family and whatever, you know. It's a rec—like, something I never thought I would do, but that's just incidental. The fact that we did it, was—and it's there, you know, you can go and watch them every week. I've want—I can't wait to tell my grandkids about—you know. What we did. Because there aren't that many great achievements in people's lives. You know, so I reckon people have none sometimes. All right, you can take our bloody community bank branch, and you can take this and you can take that, and you nationalise this and you can stuff that up, but you can't take this... There's the line and it's drawn now and it's about fucking time that someone drew the line, but it's drawn, you know, and I think—it will certainly give me a belief—a core belief that things can be achieved, but it—you know, I mean, I said beforehand and, and I would—I would say it now, that I don't have the time to do as much as I would like... ah, and I don't, but somehow with this it was so important to the cause, so much, that I made the time, you know, and did it. But also, I mean, there was no football, so, you know, I had the time. I didn't have to go to the footy every week.

ROGER HARVEY: How did I feel the day the—when the—? The day that Souths got back in I was here.

PLAYER: Roger Harvey.

ROGER: One of the nurses come and told me, it was a male one, came and told me—did I hear about Souths, he said. 'No, were they back in?', I said. He said, 'They're back in'. I said, 'I haven't heard'. So I—that's all right, here we go for next year, so that was all right. Yes, I was excited, yes. I marched into the dining room at lunch time, at... ah, lunch time. Because it was my day off, I—wouldn't have been able to hear it had I been at work. It was lunch time in the dining room. No, no, I can't—I—I—no, no. I know I didn't shout out, but I think everybody had heard about it as well.

ROBERT CORRA: That was probably one of our best ever shows I think... ah, because we just went straight to calls.

PLAYER: Robert Corra. 2SER-FM.

ROBERT: Ah, people were just absolutely elated. We had people, you know, a guy sort of, like, rang up and sort of—he didn't know what to say, he sort of said, 'Oh, I'm just so happy, I don't know how to explain', and I sort of said to him, I said, 'What... ah, when you heard that the—', he was listening on radio and he sort of said—I said, 'I bet you just smiled', and he said, 'Yes, that was it, that's exactly what I did, I just smiled, a big smile just broke out on my face'.

EILEEN MCLAUGHLIN: The only good memory of that fightback time was when we had the three judges and two of them voted us back.

PLAYER: Eileen McLaughlin.

EILEEN: All the other was hard. But people were sending in donations, so we knew it wasn't hopeless. Because if people thought it was over they wouldn't be throwing money after it. News Limited. Hate the bastards. Don't buy their papers. Wouldn't get Foxtel. George says you've got to forgive and forget. My son says, 'Geez, you're nasty, Mum, you don't forgive, do you?', and I said, 'Nup'. But I've got nothing against anybody wants to go out and buy the *Telegraph* or get Foxtel. I won't.

ERIC SIMMS: I—I was at work. We were all watching the TV—as a matter of fact, in one of our breaks.

PLAYER: Eric Simms.

ERIC: Yeah, and when they come up we were just—everything, it just erupted, yes, everyone was elated that they got back in, you know. It was the greatest thing we ever—greatest thing since we've been winning Grand Finals, I suppose, yeah, so—

ANDREW DENTON: In the case of the people versus the juggernaut, the people won.

PLAYER: Andrew Denton.

ANDREW: You know, 1999/2000, the people won. That's a precedent, you know, I think it's… um, it's really important and I—that's what I think continues to echo.

Look, it was a great day, and what can you say, it was a total vindication of, of what was right, and to their credit, News Limited were, I mean they had—again it was the smart thing to do, but they were gracious and basically said, 'Well done, great fight, let's start again on Monday', which is good.

From left: Alex Sideratos as Robert Corra, Russell Kiefel as Norm Lipson and Wayne Blair as Eric Simms in the 2004 Company B production. (Photo: Heidrun Löhr)

NICHOLAS PAPPAS: The Full Bench was in May 2001 and the decision handed down on the sixth of July.

PLAYER: Nicholas Pappas.

NICHOLAS: The Full Bench, by majority, found that Souths' exclusion contravened the Trade Practices Act because it had the effect of lessening competition.

I found out I was more resilient than I thought I was. Which I didn't think. I thought I was quite a brittle… always thought I was very sentimental, brittle, cry easily, all those sort of things, right, I cry in movies all the time, all those sort of things, y'know, my wife's sort of sitting there and I'm the one who's got the handkerchief and… um… but… er… I found out that I was more resilient than I thought I was. I also found out that I was more… y'know, we always talk about public good and having a public conscience… um, but we don't do very much about it. So I did see it as an opportunity to say to my children or my grandchildren, one day, that day I did do something good out of Law. Because Law doesn't do much good… you're an advocate for a particular client's case, and clients are very… I know lawyers get the blame, but lawyers are doing what the client wants, usually. So you're advocating someone's cause. You're a mercenary. Putting it bluntly. You're fighting someone else's war. It's not your war. And… um, but this was a war for me. It was actually me.

And everything we said in the case has happened: Optus and Foxtel are now effectively one. All the fight was for nothing. All the fight was for nothing! The decimation of Rugby League was for nothing.

We won the case on the sixth of July. Of course, we celebrated very hard that weekend. On the following Friday my father passed away. And I didn't know that on the Friday when we were in court he'd got the news that his cancer had really progressed and he didn't tell me and I rang and told him the news of the victory and all that and he was really happy and congratulated me and we were on this incredible high and then, bang, the other side of life, real life, hits you and you realise and it puts everything in perspective again… because we talk about these things and they're really important, but if your loved ones are dying around you it's not so… he wasn't expecting to pass away within a week... and... but his words on the phone... they were something like, 'You've done a good thing for the community'... 'cause that's what I was thinking and here was it being reinforced by my father and then he disappears. He was well, he was up and about. Then I was in court and he was being admitted to hospital.

It would have been George and me that would have been left standing there holding the baby if it had all come crashing down. It's a frightening thought. I think about it sometimes. And it really frightens me because inevitably there would have been some recriminations and... er... it was a burden off the shoulders. It was a feeling of lightness, of floating...

If you want me to be honest, the best moment for me was when I finally came back home. Going up the steps after a really long night, I don't think it was that late because we were exhausted, but I think it was about eleven o'clock we got home... going up the steps of my house and the door opening and it was my son and with his... I think he had his Souths scarf on, and he said, and he called out down the steps, 'We're going to the footy, Dad, we're going to the footy'. Just like that and, you know, without sounding too sentimental, but it's true. That meant everything. It was that lovely full stop. Now I didn't know that a few days later his grandfather would leave us, which would sort of deflate everything again, but... it was all very much part of the whole thing for me.

I remember at my father's funeral, last thing I would have expected, some days later, the front row on the other side of the pews, you know, all South Sydney, colours everywhere, you know, my father would never have dreamt that in his life. The South Sydney wreath was laid on his... 'cause everyone was still on a high... and all the South Sydney supporters came to this funeral. And George was there in the front row with me, and a few years ago I would have thought that absurd, this hero. So, you know... really strange.

They asked me, when the team runs on, would you like George, little George, my son, to lead them out for their first game back? And I thought about it, I thought... y'see, while I've been a Rugby League supporter all my life, I'm not really a Rugby League player-type, I've always been more towards soccer, cricket, and so I thought... 'Do I want little George in that... sort of scene?'. But then I thought, 'Yeah, it's the right thing... give him that chance'... I thought, 'It's going to be a huge moment, it's going to be broadcast all over the place. It's going to be a big buzz for him, he's going to walk down that tunnel and be the first into that manic crowd, that cauldron.' Well, he's done it... he now leads them on every game, he's now the head ball boy.

JOHN HARTIGAN: The reinstatement of Souths was a decision that was made by News Limited executive team.

PLAYER: John Hartigan.

JOHN: Lachlan Murdoch is Executive Chairman of News and he's involved in all the decision making so he was involved in that... and I think it was important that we responded quickly so that there wasn't any degree of instability or procrastination from us. And we did so. I think that the fight had been fought and it was time to get on with life.

Soon after the decision I received a card, and on the cover it says, 'Many thanks to you', and it says, 'Dear Mr Hartigan, I'm not sure what part you played with my mighty Rabbitohs', with mighty Rabbitohs underscored, 'being welcomed back to the NRL competition, but whatever you did I thank you very much. You won't regret having the mighty Rabbitohs back.' And it says, [*with a laugh*] 'Now I can buy the *Daily Telegraph* again, now I can connect to Foxtel and visit the Fox Studios. Now I can watch the *Footy Show* again and, most of all, now I can go along to the footy and watch my beloved Rabbitohs. Best wishes from Tara, with a kiss, Red and Green forever.' Now that's terrific and that was just a delight in receiving it.

And there were quite a few of those. I think that shows that from Tara's point of view, and from mine, the right outcome was reached.

GEORGE PIGGINS: Well, I—well, I felt sorry for people probably.

PLAYER: George Piggins.

GEORGE: I probably felt sorry for the Souths people more than what I did myself because I believe that in life I'm lucky enough to have other things and I was going to be able to have some sort of life after football, and some of those people haven't got anything after football, and that was probably a worry to me, that I thought that there was a lot of people there from one year to the next, all they do is care about their football side and their club, and I thought they've taken something off those people that haven't got nothing and therefore, you know, they're overstepping their mark as far as what they're doing. They didn't give those people any consideration. In the end of the day, they didn't want someone like a South Sydney football side to beat them, and even now, today, even though they've appealed in the High Court, they still don't want us to have that victory over them.

JOHN HARTIGAN: We had a finding that we contravened Trade Practices Law.

PLAYER: John Hartigan.

JOHN: And that for a company is a very critical and serious matter. All we want to do is set the record straight that we don't break laws. The finding for us, our win in the High Court, has no way of manifesting in any way to affect the club or the fans, it's purely an issue that we want to prove to ourselves that we are a law-abiding company that abides by Company Law and Trade Practices Law.

GEORGE: We've had the victory, it's ours. I don't care, you know, they can never take it off us.

PETER MACOURT: Tradition is one of those things.

PLAYER: Peter Macourt, of News Limited.

PETER: Like all sport… it's emotional. And it's difficult to reconcile the emotional side of sport to the professional side of sport. And it's there. It's unambiguously there. But. It's difficult in professional sport. It's one of those imponderables. How do you separate emotion from sport, you know? You can't. And you certainly don't want to separate emotion from sport. That's what it is. But how do you reconcile that with the commercial professional sport?… Which is about being the best, the most compelling, the most interesting, the most exciting rather than being the most traditional.

PLAYER: The Courtney family.

FREYA: I only sort of like football.

ANYA: She's coming last in the tipping competition.

BRONTE: No, she's doing all right now.

CINDY HAWKEY: We have a family tipping competition.

FREYA: Sometimes… [*long pause*] I like… [*long pause*] just going to see the game. I've got this red t-shirt that's got a little Souths thing in the middle, we've all got one, and it says, 'My daddy follows the Rabbitohs, now I can too. Thanks Uncle George.' And sometimes I wear that with a jacket and some jeans.

ANYA: Sometimes when I'm angry, I say, 'Why couldn't you bring us up following a winning team?'. Something like that.

MARK COURTNEY: The future is very promising. It's got to be promising.

PLAYER: Mark Courtney.

MARK: I—I feel—I always feel very hopeful about next season, you know, I believe, I do believe, now especially, I believe it's—I will see them in the Grand Final, I will. It will be mine. I want it, you know. It seems—I have an interesting emotion on Grand Final day which is—it's—and it's a—it's a longing, it's not so much a jealousy of the—you know, at the end, when everyone's whooping it up and the fans are—you know, it's just—it's an aching, a longing to have that—to be there and to do that… Every year, every year, yeah. And I think—Yeah, yeah, it's just this ache, I feel that I deserve it, I feel that it's in my destiny and it will be mine. So if it occurs, I—I may then have to just jump off the Gap or something [*with a laugh*] because there will be no—no—no. Life will never be that good again.

He laughs.

THE END

*From left, standing: Tyler Coppin as Roger Harvey, Eliza Logan,
Alex Sideratos (background), Jody Kennedy, Julie Hamilton
(partially obscured) and Georgina Naidu as Players; seated:
Russell Kiefel and Josef Ber as Players in the 2004 Company B
production. (Photo: Heidrun Löhr)*

For a full list of our titles, visit our website:

www.currency.com.au

Currency Press
The performing arts publisher
PO Box 2287
Strawberry Hills NSW 2012
Australia
enquiries@currency.com.au
Tel: (02) 9319 5877
Fax: (02) 9319 3649